Precious Moments Last Forever

Laura C. Martin

Collector Portraits by
Carolyn Jones

Abbeville Press Publishers
New York London Paris

 First edition.

Editor: Alice Gray

Creative Director: Diane Gebert

Production Supervisor: Dana Cole

Project Director: Linda Masterson

Photography by:
Big Deahl Productions, Inc.
Enesco Corporation Photography Studio
Graphic Arts Productions
GSP Marketing Services, Inc.
Rockafellow Photography Inc.
Pettersen & Associates
Laura Straus
Color Separations: Tukaiz Innovative Prepress

Library of Congress Cataloging-in-Publication Data

Martin. Laura C.
Precious moments last forever / Laura C. Martin.
p. cm.
Includes index.
ISBN 1-55959-859-6
1. Precious Moments, Inc. 2. Porcelain figures—Missouri—History—20th century. 3. Inspiration—Religious aspects—Collectibles. I. Title.
NK4210.P73M37 1994
738.8'2'097731—dc20

94-27040

Printed and bound in the USA

Contents

Beginnings

The Collectors and the Collection

The Precious Moments Community

The Precious Moments Chapel

The Precious Moments Collection

HOLY BIBLE

PERFECT
HARMONY

Left to right:
Gene Freedman
Sam Butcher
Yasuhei Fujioka

The story of Precious Moments is the story of our lives, of the experiences, both ordinary and meaningful, that mark each of our days. Much more than a history of porcelain figurines, this is also the tale of three highly creative people: Sam Butcher, an artist inspired by his faith; Gene Freedman, a businessman working in the giftware industry who recognized the potential popularity of Sam's artwork; and Yasuhei Fujioka, a Japanese sculptor who transformed Sam's wonderful drawings into magical, three-dimensional messengers of love and hope.

At the heart of the Precious Moments story are "just folks," people who have written by the thousands to Sam Butcher to thank him for the joy the figurines have given and the wonderful memories they represent.

In 1975 Sam Butcher was a young artist with enormous faith and a small pocketbook. Recognizing the need for visual aids in the Christian teaching field, he started a greeting card company with a partner, William Biel. They called their small enterprise "Jonathan and David" in honor of the celebrated friendship and faith of the biblical Jonathan and Prince David. When asked to participate in the 1975 Christian Booksellers Association convention, Sam and Bill prepared a line of cards and posters entitled Precious Moments.

From the very beginning, what made these cards and posters so unique—and eventually, so popular—were their special, inspirational messages; they became the vehicle through which Sam and Bill shared their faith with countless others.

The response to the cards and posters was tremendous, but Sam and Bill wanted to do more; they wanted to transform the line into porcelain bisque. Lacking adequate finances and expertise in the porcelain field, their vision remained only a dream until early in 1978, when Eugene Freedman first spotted Precious Moments artwork.

"Basically they are the offspring of a spiritual love for other people," Sam said of the first Precious Moments cards he designed.

Original poster courtesy of Precious Insights *magazine.*

"I could sense that the Precious Moments artwork was everything they had in the world. It was like their own children," Gene Freedman said of his first conversation with Sam and Bill.

Eugene Freedman, president of Enesco Corporation, is considered a pioneer in the giftware industry. While traveling to Asia in the spring of 1978, Gene stopped in southern California to attend the Los Angeles Gift Show.

In Enesco's L.A. showroom, a friend brought him a poster of two little boys with big, soulful eyes. One carried a fishing pole, the other a can of worms; it was titled *I Will Make You Fishers Of Men*. Instantly, Gene Freedman fell in love with the little fishermen and with Precious Moments. He asked to see more.

Gene knew immediately that this warm, tender drawing of two teardrop-eyed children was truly special and would be even more so when translated into porcelain. He was eager to meet the people behind Precious Moments.

When Gene called Sam and Bill, they were initially reluctant to talk to him, as they were still hoping to have the artwork made into porcelain themselves; they were uncertain that anyone else could really share their commitment to creating artworks that conveyed messages of devotion and inspiration. Fortunately, Gene was gently persistent.

Eventually, Sam and Bill agreed to come to Chicago and meet with Gene Freedman. There was something about Gene that struck them as different, as undeniably sincere. "He seemed very serious and very appreciative of the artwork," Sam recalled, "He really seemed to care."

That first meeting, which lasted several hours, proved to be a profoundly important experience for all three men, for they quickly recognized each other as kindred souls. They spoke not only of art and porcelain, but of family, faith, and matters of the spirit.

But Gene knew that talking alone would not convince Sam and Bill that their pastel illustrations could be beautifully and lovingly transformed into porcelain. He realized he would have to prove it to them with an actual figurine.

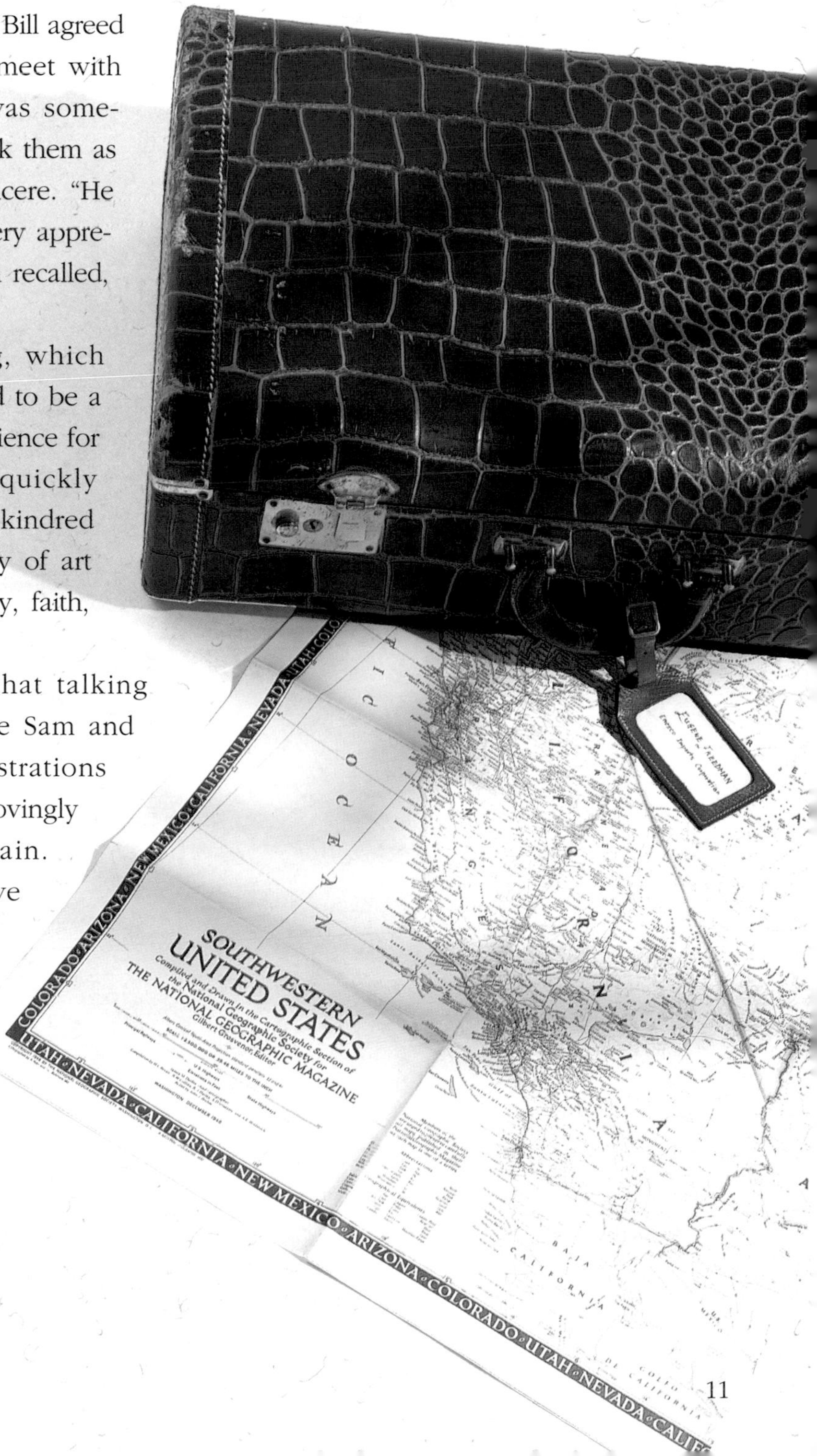

The proper choice of sculptors was crucial to the success of the Precious Moments project. Gene Freedman knew exactly who he wanted: master sculptor Yasuhei Fujioka from Nagoya, Japan, who had worked with him for over twenty years. Gene sensed intuitively that his friend and colleague Fujioka-san (in Japan, "san" is added to a person's name as a sign of respect) would understand how special the Precious Moments drawings were and would treat them with the tender reverence they deserved.

He entrusted Fujioka-san with one of Sam's drawings of a little boy and girl sitting on a tree stump, titled *Love One Another*. With deliberate care and great skill, the sculptor molded it into the first Precious Moments figurine.

When it was finished, Gene was so pleased and excited about the figurine, he called Sam and Bill and asked them to meet him in Chicago to see it.

A few of the tools used to sculpt a prototype figurine.

At Enesco headquarters just outside of Chicago in Elk Grove Village, Illinois, Sam and Bill watched as Gene carefully unwrapped the porcelain piece he had carried from the design studio in Japan.

When Gene presented Sam with *Love One Another*, Sam sank to his knees, cradled the figurine in his hands, and said, "Look, Bill, look!"

The three men passed the figurine back and forth, awed by how Fujioka-san's craft and sensitivity had transformed Sam's pastel children into a three-dimensional artwork, still brimming with all the emotion and expression of the original concept.

For the first time, Sam and Bill began to believe that something magical was happening, but they still hesitated and asked to take the figurine back home to think it over. Gene agreed, but requested an additional twenty drawings to take to Japan to be made into porcelain.

Within a few days Sam called to say they loved the figurine, but wanted to work directly with the sculptor. Immediately, arrangements were made for Sam and Bill to fly to Japan.

"I can't tell you how proud we are to be presenting Sam's artwork in porcelain. It's an honor we don't take lightly," Gene Freedman said during the development of the first Precious Moments figurines.

Love One Another *was the very first Precious Moments figurine sculpted.*

"*When I meet with Fujioka-san, it is as though we go off into our own little world.*"

— *Sam Butcher*

Fujioka-san spoke no English and Sam Butcher spoke no Japanese, but through the universal language of art, these two men developed a more effective means of communicating than any words could match. During that first trip to Japan, Sam and Fujioka-san spent hours together working with a sketch pad, until sculptor and artist related, in Sam's words, "heart to heart." Their close communication resulted in the translation of numerous drawings into porcelain bisque; each figurine was handcrafted to retain the original spirit of Sam's illustrations.

In the fall of 1978, twenty-one Precious Moments figurines, each one handcrafted and individually painted, were introduced on the market.

The original twenty-one Precious Moments figurines were: *A.* Unto Us A Child Is Born, *B.* Jesus Is Born, *C.* His Burden Is Light, *D.* Come Let Us Adore Him, *E.* Love Lifted Me, *F.* Jesus Is The Answer, *G.* Make A Joyful Noise, *H.* Prayer Changes Things, *I.* He Leadeth Me, *J.* We Have Seen His Star, *K.* Jesus Is The Light, *L.* Jesus Loves Me *(boy), M.* Jesus Loves Me *(girl), N.* Love One Another, *O.* God Understands, *P.* Smile God Loves You, *Q.* God Loveth A Cheerful Giver, *R.* Love Is Kind, *S.* O, How I Love Jesus, *T.* He Careth For You, *and U.* Praise The Lord Anyhow.

The response from the first people who bought the figurines was unusually personal and very moving.

They wrote that their Precious Moments had touched their lives and been able to uniquely express what was in their hearts. The figurines reminded them of a child, a friend, a loved one, or of a meaningful time or event.

After only one year public demand for the figurines was overwhelming.

Although thrilled by the response, Sam and Gene never lost sight of the original purpose of Precious Moments: to create artworks that communicate heartfelt emotion and abiding faith.

The collection now numbers over 1,000. New introductions are often sold before they even arrive at authorized dealers. Sam's creativity seems boundless. And all three "fathers" of the collection—Sam, Gene, and Fujioka-san—are steadfast in their loyalty to the integrity of the collection and their belief in living the Collector's Club motto of "Loving, Caring, and Sharing." Perhaps that is why today Precious Moments figurines are one of the most popular collectibles in the world.

Sam Butcher
The Creator

All who know him say they are richer for the experience. All who have met him come away smiling. All who have seen his art and read his words of inspiration know that he is someone very special.

Samuel Butcher, the creator of Precious Moments, is a man with a big heart, a ready smile, and many talents. And yet, as successful as he is, Sam is still a humble spirit, full of steadfast faith and great love for all the people he has influenced with his artwork.

Friends say that Sam has a sixth sense about what people need, and this comes through in every drawing he makes. He has great compassion, and he innately understands the joy and hardship that are an integral part of every life.

Sam's own life has been filled with tough times and good times, happy celebrations and deep sorrows. These very human, very familiar moments have guided him in his creation of Precious Moments.

"To know Sam is to understand why so many have been touched and changed by the wonderful influence of his Precious Moments children and their messages of Loving, Caring, and Sharing."

— Gene Freedman

Above left: One of Sam's most vivid childhood memories is of his mother making bib overalls out of flour sacks for the boys.
Above right: The Butcher brothers and sister with their mom: Sam, Hank, Chuck, Dawn, and Ray.
Bottom left: Young Sam with his grade-school classmates. Sam is in the top row on the far left.

Sam's high school art teacher, Rex Moravec, encouraged Sam to pursue an art career. He inspired the figurine I Can't Spell Success Without You.

I Can't Spell Success Without You

One of Sam's earliest paintings, done with the only art supplies he had—automotive paints.

Sam's early years were not easy ones. From the very beginning, Sam felt separate from his family. Unlike his father and his brothers, he was not interested in motorcycles and cars, preferring to spend his time drawing and writing stories. Sam decided at an early age he wanted to be an artist, but his father opposed this decision.

Sam found support elsewhere though; one of the most influential people in his early life was his high school art teacher, Rex Moravec. "He was a talented man who had the unique ability to bring out the best in his students," said Sam.

When Samuel John Butcher graduated from Redding High School in Redding, California in 1958, he was full of hopes and dreams. He wrote his mother a note on the back of his graduation picture, telling her that he hoped someday she would be proud of him. Unfortunately, his mother did not live long enough to see Sam's first Precious Moments drawings.

I'm Sending You A White Christmas

Above: Sam's mother, Evelyn Mae, always believed her son would "do something wonderful."
Left: I'm Sending You A White Christmas *was specially created in memory of Sam's mother. She had moved to Michigan from Florida when she was five years old. When it snowed at Christmas, she made snowballs and tried to send them to her friends back in Florida.*

Sam's dream of becoming an artist finally came true when he went to work for the Child Evangelism Fellowship.

After he finished high school, Sam won a scholarship to the College of Arts and Crafts in Berkeley, California. In 1959 he married Katie Cushman and they moved into a tiny apartment located near the college. Money was short, but love was abundant. Sam and Katie were happy, even as they stretched to make ends meet.

In March 1962 Sam came home to be with Katie for the birth of their first child, Jon. He never went back to college and worked odd jobs to support his small family.

During these lean years, Katie and Sam began attending North Valley Church, an experience that had a tremendous impact on Sam's life. He began to study the Bible, and soon he dedicated his life to the Lord. His faith led him to the Child Evangelism Fellowship (CEF) in Grand Rapids, Michigan, where he went to work first in the shipping office, and later, in the art department.

As his family continued to grow (by 1969, the Butchers had six children: Jon, Philip, Tammy, Debbie, Timmy, and Donnie), Sam continued to work for CEF and it was here that he met Bill Biel.

Sam and Bill founded Jonathan and David, Inc., in Grand Rapids, Michigan, to create artwork with heartfelt messages of devotion and inspiration.

This original painting of Jonathan and David was created by the artist Sam Butcher and hung in the Jonathan and David building in Grand Rapids, Michigan. The size of the original was approximately six feet by six feet. The painting illustrates the Old Testament story in which Prince Jonathan willingly relinquishes his crown and power to David.

Both Sam and Bill worked at CEF before deciding to go out on their own as commercial artists and form the Jonathan and David partnership.

From the very start, they wanted their products to fill a special niche. But as orders for Precious Moments cards and posters steadily increased, the partners weren't completely satisfied; they dreamed of doing more.

When Gene Freedman of Enesco called Sam and Bill to say he wanted to make Precious Moments into porcelain figurines, they were initially reluctant to talk to him. They were uncertain that anyone else could really share their commitment to creating artworks that conveyed messages of devotion and inspiration. Fortunately, Gene was gently persistent. It was really the start of a magical journey.

"We imagined that these porcelain figurines, fashioned after my artwork, would be little messengers delivering the inspirational thoughts and teachings of the Lord. They would be, in fact, our ministry," remembers Sam.

When Bill eventually decided to devote himself full-time to Jonathan and David, Inc., Sam began working even more closely with Enesco. Their long and fruitful relationship is based on a shared vision and a common dedication to the mission and spirit of Precious Moments.

Daughter Debbie's loving nature is a frequent source of inspiration for Sam.

Sam continues to work tirelessly with Enesco and the Precious Moments line. A man of boundless energy, he seems to go non-stop from one project to the next, his mind full of ideas and dreams and visions. Sam says that his inspiration comes from his faith, his ideas from friends and family.

Sam's daughter, Debbie, was the model for *God Loveth A Cheerful Giver,* which was based on Debbie's rescue of a box full of kittens who were about to be put to sleep. This piece, which was retired in 1981, is now one of the most sought-after figurines on the Precious Moments secondary market, commanding hundreds and sometimes thousands of dollars.

When the figurine first appeared it incorrectly read, "Free Puppiess." This was quickly fixed, but those first figurines bearing the mistake are highly prized by collectors—as much for their rarity as for their resale value.

God Loveth A Cheerful Giver

"Precious Moments are conceived in the heart, not on the drawing board. I use children as the subject matter because I feel they are the purest expression of innocence."

— Sam Butcher

"God's gift to me was a lesson that Precious Moments are born out of happiness and sorrow, so that having experienced the height and depth of both, I am able to create the things that touch and minister to others."
—Sam Butcher

Going Home

Not all of Sam's inspirations are happy ones, for Sam has had his own share of heartache. One of the darkest periods of his life came when his son Philip was killed in an automobile accident in 1990. The loss of his son was devastating, and Sam spent many hours praying for guidance and looking to friends and family for support.

"I was overseas when I heard about my son's death," Sam remembers. "Just one phone call, and my son was gone. I couldn't believe it. I thought, 'Dear God, how am I ever going to get through this, what am I going to do?' "

Sam put his heart and mind to work creating a piece in honor of his beloved child, *Going Home*, which is now one of the most cherished in the collection. The happy, "heaven-bound" figure recalls Philip's cheerful wit and zest for life. "God's gift to me was a lesson that Precious Moments are born out of happiness and sorrow, so that having experienced the height and depth of both, I am able to create the things that touch and minister to others," says Sam.

Collector Melanie Matsumoto wrote: "When Sam Butcher introduced *Going Home* as a tribute to his son, I thought it was really cute. It wasn't until my own friend was killed in a car accident that I treasured this piece dearly. Nothing can ever replace my friend, but this special figurine will always fill my heart with memories and especially 'precious moments' of my dear friend."

"*I will never forget the day I saw Fujioka-san's sculpture of* To God Be The Glory *in his studio. It was altogether lovely. It was the story of my life! For any success that I have enjoyed is not a coincidence, nor is it the result of talent alone. The Lord is good and has blessed my work."*

— Sam Butcher

When asked about his personal favorite figurine, Sam has a difficult time responding. "My favorite changes all the time . . . but I must say that the one that has meant the most to me is *Jesus Is The Answer.* There are many people who have no answers to problems in this world. Perhaps this will prompt them to help others."

Another of Sam's favorites is *To God Be The Glory,* which was inspired by Psalm 29:2, "Give unto the Lord the glory due unto His name . . ."

From the very start, Sam's goal was to reach people and to help them when he could. Describing his years with Jonathan and David, Inc., he wrote: "The cards were the product of a ministry that was rather personal. Through the years there were many people who had problems in their lives and needed someone to tell them 'I'm here if you need me.'"

And Sam is still here for those who need him. His "little messengers" have found their way into hearts and homes from the White House on Pennsylvania Avenue to a small apartment in Harlem. Everywhere they are loved.

To God Be The Glory

Jesus Is The Answer

Sam Butcher truly loves people, and often takes time to stop and talk to collectors or sign a favorite figurine.

It is Sam's humanity that makes him so enormously popular as both an artist and a speaker. Every year tens of thousands of visitors come to the magnificent chapel Sam built near Carthage, Missouri, seeking to share their faith and hoping to get a glimpse of the creator of Precious Moments.

Though inspired by the divine, Sam has a very human touch. One day as he left the chapel, he came across a woman with a car full of children. She was trying to fix a flat tire with a jack that didn't fit, so he stopped and offered to help. The family had just been to the chapel, and Sam asked how they had liked it. The woman said they loved it, though the artist had so many visitors around him, they had not even been able to see him.

Sam grinned, and said that they were looking at him now. The woman was amazed and asked why someone as important and busy as Sam would stop to change a tire. Laughing, Sam answered, "Because it was flat!"

Collectors throughout the country think of Sam as a family member. They write him volumes of letters telling him how Precious Moments have touched their lives, they stand in line for hours to have him sign a figurine, and drive hundreds of miles to visit the chapel he created.

And Sam never disappoints them. Even though he has been blessed with tremendous worldly success, he has kept his sense of humor and his love and compassion for all people.

"I am grateful to have played a part in bringing the world the Precious Moments messages of Loving, Caring, and Sharing."

— Gene Freedman

Eugene Freedman
The Discoverer

"The best is yet to come!" Anyone who knows Gene Freedman, or G.F., as he is affectionately called, has heard these words over and over again. It is Gene's motto, and a declaration of his unwavering optimism about his favorite topic, the Precious Moments figurines.

His office is a gallery that illustrates his life. The walls and desk are crowded with photographs of friends and family, special presentations from civic leaders and statesmen, and figurines of particular significance.

Gene's official title is President and Chief Executive Officer of the Enesco Worldwide Giftware Group. Under his enthusiastic leadership, the company has climbed to the top of the giftware industry and Gene has enjoyed great personal and professional success, all of which he has been quick to share.

Gene's generosity is legendary; he uses both his financial resources and his position of influence to reach out to those less fortunate.

Gene Freedman has won awards and accolades from Ellis Island to the White House. As generous with his praise as he is with his success, Gene credits his parents Ethel and Isadore Freedman with helping him to develop the values and principles that have shaped his life.

Ethel and Isadore were Russian Jews who came to America early in the 1900s. They met and married in Philadelphia and had three children. Soon after Gene was born in 1925, the family moved to Milwaukee.

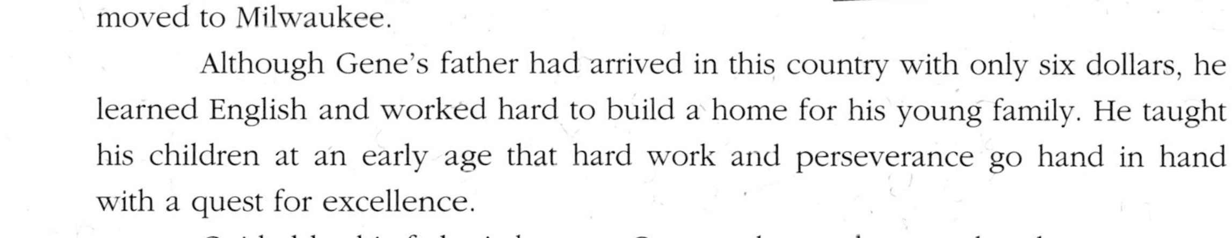

Although Gene's father had arrived in this country with only six dollars, he learned English and worked hard to build a home for his young family. He taught his children at an early age that hard work and perseverance go hand in hand with a quest for excellence.

Guided by his father's lessons, Gene understood even when he was young that good fortune is a blessing not to be taken for granted, a philosophy he has lived by throughout his life.

Clockwise from top photo: Young Gene (on left) with his dad and brother, Marty; with his mom and dad; learning to drive his first car; and with his big brother, Marty.

"Whoever and whatever I am today, it is because of these two wonderful role models and the values they instilled in me."

— Gene Freedman

After studying oceanography at the California Institute of Technology, Gene received his naval commission at Notre Dame Midshipman's School, and later served as an officer in Guam.

Like other immigrant families, the Freedmans were fiercely proud of their American citizenship and when World War II began, Gene, then a freshman at Northwestern University, enlisted in the navy.

After his discharge from the navy, Gene returned to Milwaukee and began working for a giftware manufacturer. Early in 1950 he left the firm to start his own business producing decorative figurines and wall decor.

Gene was now a busy family man, supporting a wife, a son, and two daughters. When the Enesco Company was being formed in 1958, he sold his own business and joined the Chicago-based importer.

Ruth and Gene Freedman on their honeymoon.

"I started the business with very little money and had to put a desk in the bedroom of my apartment. To make it sound more official, I called it 'Suite 306.'"

—Gene Freedman

The Freedman family, clockwise from left: Penny, Gene, Ruth, Rick, De De the poodle, and Nancy.

The flags of Enesco and Precious Moments proudly flank the American flag at company headquarters outside Chicago.

Gene was determined to do his best with the new company. By the late 1970s Enesco became an industry leader and Gene was regarded as a trendsetter.

Certainly one of the most exciting moments in his business career was that day in 1978 when he first saw Sam Butcher's drawings of beautiful children bearing messages of inspiration and hope. Gene's instinctive response to the Precious Moments drawings convinced him of the vast potential of these artworks. Time has proven he was right.

Through Gene's creative management, the Precious Moments line has become important to thousands of people all over the globe. First introduced as giftware, growing demand for the figurines soon elevated the line to collectible status.

The success of the Precious Moments Collection has helped Gene Freedman and Enesco reach higher and higher. But remembering the lessons of his youth, Gene has never forgotten those whom fortune has overlooked. When the Precious Moments Collectors' Club first formed in 1981, he turned to a small workshop for disabled adults called Opportunity, Inc., employing the participants to assemble and mail information kits to new Collectors' Club members. The partnership between Enesco and adults with disabilities continues today.

"I am pleased that I have been able to give something back to humanity. We don't help others with the idea that we will receive an honor or an award. For me, as for most people, the reward is what we feel when we see that our efforts have been able to touch and improve the lives of others."
—Gene Freedman

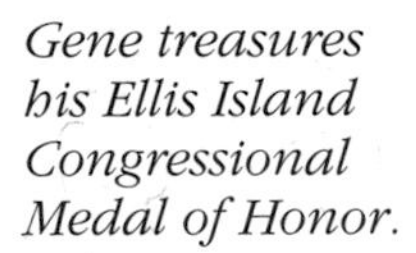

Gene treasures his Ellis Island Congressional Medal of Honor.

Eugene Freedman,
President and C.E.O. of Enesco.

Gene Freedman's philanthropic efforts have not gone unnoticed. In 1989 the Media Access Committee of California honored him with an award for excellence in aiding and supporting the employment of persons with disabilities.

The mayor of Milwaukee and the governor of Wisconsin declared September 11, 1990 "Eugene Freedman Day" in recognition of his efforts to "improve the quality of life for the people of Wisconsin."

In 1991 Gene and Sam were invited to a breakfast reception at the White House, where they presented President and Mrs. George Bush with a special Precious Moments figurine *God Bless The U.S.A.*, dedicated to the National Day of Prayer.

And on April 26, 1992, the National Ethnic Coalition of Organizations presented Eugene Freedman with an Ellis Island Congressional Medal of Honor. This coveted award honors the recipient's individual achievements as well as his heritage.

Of the many people Gene has known in his life, his parents have always been his greatest influence and inspiration. They left him a rich heritage, a strong sense of community, an appreciation of the importance of a job well done, and an awareness of the needs of others. It is a legacy that Gene Freedman lives each day.

Gene's efforts have enriched the lives of many, and his example is a living testament to his values and faith.

Gene's relationship with Enesco, and especially with Sam Butcher, has played a pivotal role in his life and career. "It's more than simply rhetoric to say that my Precious Moments association over these two decades has had a profound effect on my entire life," says Gene, "beginning with my friendship with Sam. I have never known a better friend or confidant, or one who has given me wiser counsel."

Sam and Fujioka-san surprised their old friend, Gene, with his own one-of-a-kind Precious Moments figurine, Maui Christmas, *because of the Freedmans' love for Hawaii.*

Maui Christmas

Yasuhei Fujioka
The Sculptor

Yasuhei Fujioka was born to a family of artisans in the town of Nagoya, Japan on December 28, 1921. His father was a landscape architect who designed parks and gardens. Even as a small boy, Yasuhei loved to draw. In high school he majored in design and after graduation, began work as a ceramics designer at a local company. Though the work was interesting, Yasuhei Fujioka yearned for more; soon he enrolled in advanced studies in sculpture.

The young artisan's training was interrupted by World War II, but after the war, he returned to the same job. In 1955 he established a design studio, and shortly thereafter, he met Gene Freedman and began his relationship with Enesco.

Twenty-three years later, when Gene discovered Sam's Precious Moments drawings, the visionary businessman knew that his beloved and trusted colleague Fujioka-san would be the perfect person to make them into porcelain, for Fujioka-san possessed the necessary combination of technical skill and artistic sensitivity required to capture the feeling of Sam's drawings.

"I always have felt, ever since I first met Fujioka-san, that we just sort of related, almost as one person. That is very, very unique."

—Sam Butcher

A man of few words, Fujioka-san prefers to let his incomparable, eloquent figurines speak for him. The transformation of Sam's drawings into three-dimensional sculptures is nothing short of breathtaking; the man who has made this possible holds magic in his fingers.

"The first time I encountered Precious Moments was when I saw the six cards sent from Enesco," Fujioka-san recalls. "I found something different in these cards compared to ones I saw at the market. I chose a few drawings and began to make figurines. I remember the enthusiasm I felt in translating these lovely children into figurines. I did not want those cards to be taken from me."

Artists often find it difficult to work with one another, but Sam and Fujioka-san were drawn to each other immediately. Fujioka-san always seems to understand exactly how to turn Sam's art into inspirational porcelain figurines.

Renowned in Japan as a master sculptor, Fujioka-san still works every day at the design studio in Nagoya. In 1977 he was joined by his son, Shuhei, who is continuing the tradition of artistry in the Fujioka family. Shuhei has also attained the venerable title of master sculptor.

"I remember the enthusiasm I felt in translating these lovely children into figurines."

—Yasuhei Fujioka

Fujioka-san continues to spend endless hours with each figurine in order to capture every detail and nuance of Sam's drawings. He is not satisfied until each figurine is perfect, and often destroys several prototypes until he is pleased with the final product.

Fujioka-san believes that the popularity of Precious Moments is an "unprecedented miracle." When asked where he receives his inspiration for the beautiful figurines he creates, he is quick to reply, "From Sam!"

Each and every one of Sam's drawings is prized by the great artisan who transforms them into sculptures. "I've been greatly influenced by all the Precious Moments figurines," says Fujioka-san. "Some of my favorites include *He Cleansed My Soul, Your Love Is So Uplifting, Going Home,* and *Sending You My Love.*"

During the past few years, in addition to his work with the design studio, Fujioka-san has taken up oil painting. He completes at least ten paintings a year and exhibits them in a small gallery in Nagoya.

One of master sculptor Yasuhei Fujioka's hobbies is oil painting.

He Cleansed My Soul

Your Love Is So Uplifting

Going Home

Sending You My Love

From Inspiration to Figurine

It takes an artist two years of training to learn to paint the eyes, but this is only one indication of the time, effort, and love that goes into creating each Precious Moments figurine.

Before the eyes are even a paint drop at the end of the brush, a great deal must be done. It can take as long as seven to ten days to craft a single piece.

From the beginning to the end of the production process, each figurine is checked at intervals by at least twelve inspectors.

If at any point in the process a flaw is detected that cannot be corrected, the figurine is destroyed. There are no Precious Moments "seconds." Every piece that goes on the market is perfect.

Even when the demand for Precious Moments figurines increased to a frenzy, Enesco refused to compromise their commitment to excellence. Instead, they launched one of the largest recruiting and artisan-training programs ever undertaken in the ceramics industry.

Maintaining the integrity of the collection has also been a consistently high priority for Enesco. Ever since the figurines were introduced, various imitations have shown up on the market. Enesco has been diligent about protecting Sam's original drawings, the figurines, and all Precious Moments items with copyright registrations.

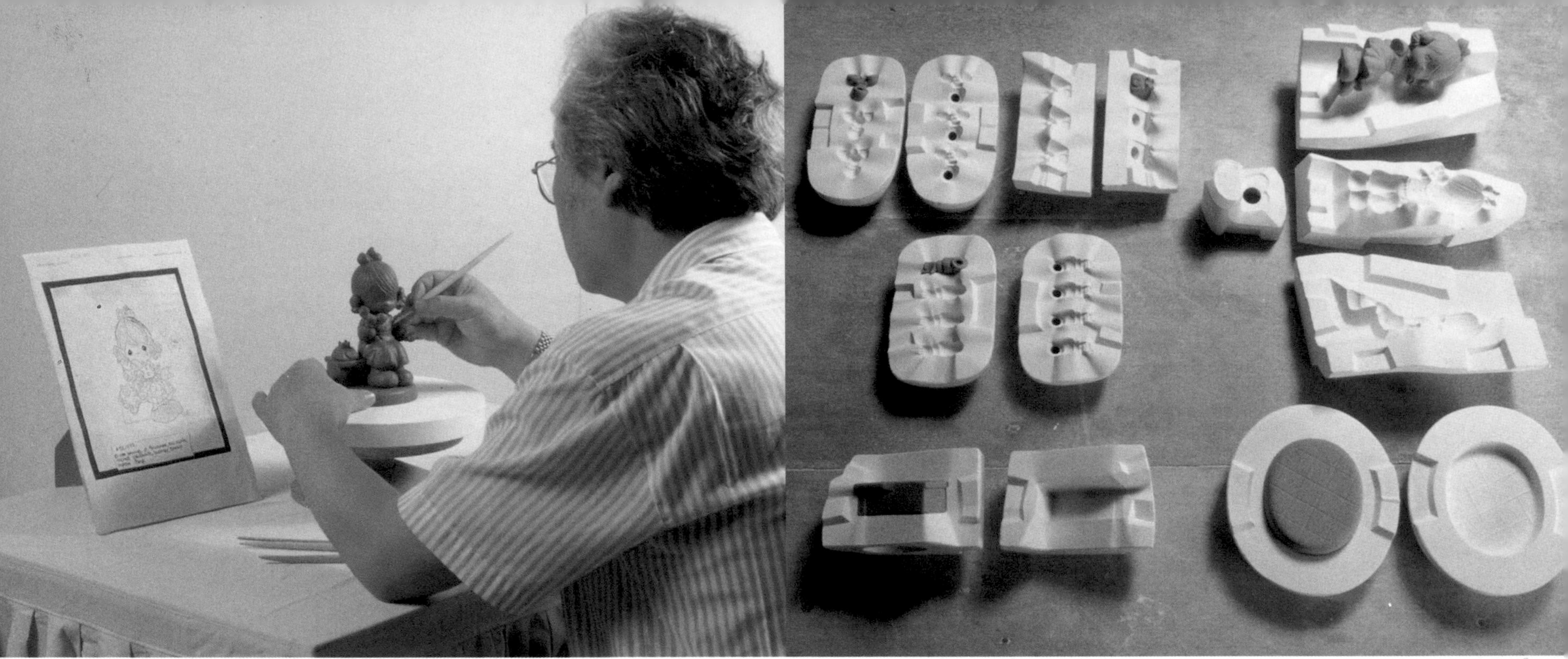

1. Working from Sam Butcher's original drawing, a sculptor, under the direction of Yasuhei Fujioka, models moist clay into the general form of the subject. Then, striving for perfection, the sculptor works the clay until a fully dimensional sculpture emerges.

2. Once the clay model is reviewed and approved, casts are made so that the original can be reproduced. Due to the complexity of the figurine designs, each model is cut into as many as a dozen different parts.

3. There are two kinds of molds produced. One is called a "case mold." The other is called a "production mold," which is produced from the case mold and is used for the actual production of figurines.

4. The pieces of the plaster mold are assembled with strong rubber straps, then a special mixture of porcelain liquid called "slip" is poured into the mold.

5. The mold absorbs the mixture and when the slip has reached a certain thickness, excess liquid is poured off. Approximately thirty minutes later, the hardened positive, called "greenware," is carefully knocked loose from the mold by an artisan.

6. The individual pieces are attached together with a mixture of the same slip from which the figurine is cast. Mold lines are smoothed away and some resculpting may be done in order to faithfully reproduce the original model.

7. The sculpture is fired for approximately fourteen hours in a gas kiln at 2300°F. After this initial firing, the greenware scupture turns brilliant white and becomes hard and durable, while still maintaining all the details and characteristics of Sam's original artwork.

8. Polishing, which primes the figurine for the painting process, is accomplished by tumbling each piece in a bath of fine pumice, much like polishing a precious jewel. This technique renders the entire surface smooth and satiny to the touch.

9. Each figurine will undergo at least six complete inspections. After polishing, each piece is intensely scrutinized before it is allowed to be painted.

10. Each figurine is painted by highly skilled artisans who work from a pastel palette of as many as sixteen colors specifically formulated to duplicate Sam's artwork. These artisans often wield four to six brushes at a time, actually bringing each figurine to life through a multi-step painting process.

11. Painted colors are fused permanently to the figurine while it is fired a second time. This firing is done in an electric "tunnel kiln" at 1300°F and takes approximately four hours.

12. Once the final painstaking inspection has been completed, infinite care is used in packing each figurine, as it will travel thousands of miles before reaching its destination.

Annual Production Marks

Year	Mark	Symbol	Meaning
1981	Triangle		Symbol of the triune — God the Father, Son, & Holy Ghost.
1982	Hourglass		Represents the time we have on earth to serve the Lord.
1983	Fish		Earliest symbol used by members of the early Christian apostolic church.
1984	Cross		Symbol of Christianity recognized worldwide.
1985	Dove		Symbol of love and peace.
1986	Olive Branch		Symbol of peace and understanding.
1987	Cedar Tree		Symbol of strength, beauty, and preservation.
1988	Flower		Represents God's love for His children.
1989	Bow & Arrow		Represents the power of the Bible.
1990	Flame		For those who have gone through the fire of life and found comfort in believing.
1991	Vessel		A reminder of God's love, which flows through the vessel of life.
1992	G-Clef		Symbolizes the harmony of God's love.
1993	Butterfly		Represents the rebirth of man, who comes from darkness into the light.
1994	Trumpet		Represents the Precious Moments message of Loving, Caring, and Sharing. The trumpet also signifies a battle cry and a heralder of victory.

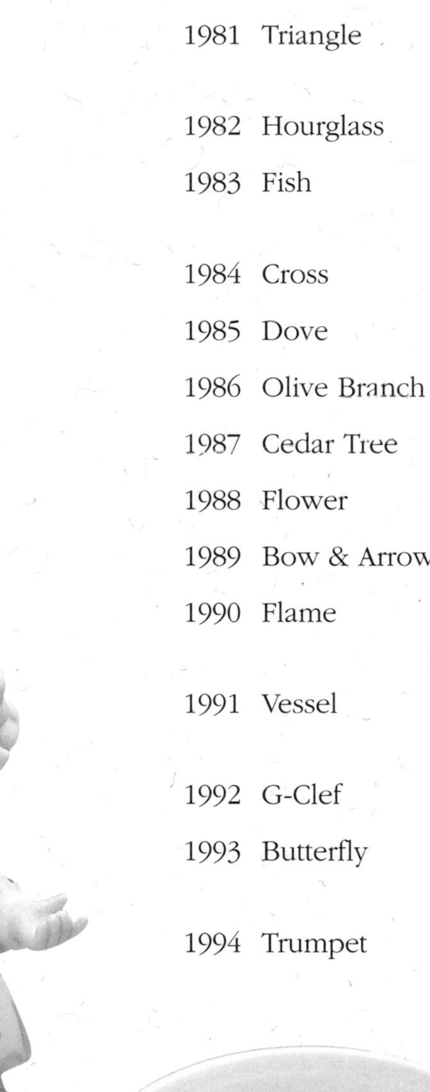

Sam was once asked why he created so many different figurines. He responded, "So each individual can relate to them in a very personal way. Choosing a figurine is like picking a special friend. I am trying to reach people on a personal level . . . to express love toward people that I don't even know. My work is really a ministry."

The Collectors and the Collection

> *The figurines have different meanings for different people.* His Eye Is On The Sparrow *reminds one collector of the family of baby birds she and her mother saved one year. To another collector, it served as a symbol that God would look after her son and his family during their missionary work in South America.*

The Enesco Precious Moments collection is made up of figurines that depict scenes so familiar we want to laugh, cry, sigh with contentment, or grin with pleasure at each one of them. The appeal of the figurines is so universal it seems to touch everyone, yet so unique that we wonder if Sam Butcher didn't create them with each of us especially in mind.

The messages and situations illustrated by Precious Moments figurines are instantly recognizable. All of us have a *Purr-fect Grandma,* a *Mother Sew Dear*, or a *Special Dad,* and all of us know that *Nobody's Perfect* and that *We Need A Good Friend Through The Ruff Times.* And it never hurts to be reminded from time to time that *The Good Lord Always Delivers*, and *Prayer Changes Things.* Sam always seems to know what is in our hearts.

There is no such thing as a "typical collector," for Precious Moments figurines speak to all kinds of people, from babies to grandparents, schoolchildren to doctors. Collectors live in apartments in the city and farmhouses in the country. They are from all fifty states and many foreign countries. Some collectors have hundreds of pieces, others only a few.

Despite the diversity of the people who collect Precious Moments figurines, the ties that bind them all are their love of the figurines and their belief in the special messages sent by Sam Butcher.

The figurines have different meanings for different people. *His Eye Is On The Sparrow* reminds one collector of the family of baby birds she and her mother saved one year. To another collector, it served as a symbol that God would look after her son and his family as they performed their missionary work in South America.

Each collector's group of figurines is uniquely significant. They represent the memories, important occasions, and milestones in his or her own life. Often they become a three-dimensional family album to be shared with loved ones time and time again.

Even more astounding than the range of collectors is the variety of the collection itself. Now numbering over 1,000, the figurines represent every imaginable occasion, and Sam is still going strong, adding new pieces to the collection every year.

Make A Joyful Noise is one of the original twenty-one figurines introduced in 1978. Sam tells a funny story about how he came up with the idea for this piece.

He and Bill Biel were driving on a country road when they came upon a woman in a car whose bumper sticker read, "Honk If You Love Jesus." So naturally, they honked. She looked up, and apparently forgetting the instructions on her bumper sticker, assumed they were rude young men; she gave them a dirty look and mouthed unprintable words.

They pointed to the bumper sticker and honked again, and the same thing happened. They finally gave up and drove away. From this episode, Sam was inspired to create an image of a little girl nose to nose with a goose. This piece was originally called *Honk If You Love Jesus*; its title was changed before production to *Make A Joyful Noise*.

Make A Joyful Noise *was originally titled* Honk If You Love Jesus. *Buttons (top) were actually produced with the original title.*

The production of the Precious Moments figurines is as close to perfect as possible, but as we all know, to err is human, and there have been some mistakes, goofs, and mix-ups over the years since the figurines were introduced. In fact, the prototype for the very first figurine, *Love One Another,* was much larger than the figurine that is now so familiar. Sam and Fujioka-san worked together to scale down the size of the figurine while preserving its beauty and impact.

Because both Sam and the Enesco team are perfectionists, there are many examples of figurines whose designs have been changed or details altered.

The original prototype of the collection, Love One Another, *was re-sculpted and re-sized several times before Sam, Gene, and Fujioka-san agreed it was perfect. The final version is on the far right.*

Nobody's Perfect was introduced in 1982. The little boy in the dunce cap was first depicted as smiling, but his face was soon corrected to show an open-mouthed, "O" expression. Of the two, the smiling boy is more rare, and thus more valuable, though the corrected version was retired in 1990, and is now highly prized as well.

Another facial alteration occurred with *Faith Takes The Plunge*. Some of the original figurines had a wide smile instead of the determined frown the corrected figurine wears.

Sometimes creative changes are made after the pieces have entered the market. A figurine made for the National Easter Seal Society was first issued as a little girl wearing a plain skirt and holding a small flower pot. Sam felt that she needed a little extra something to be more in keeping with a colorful and lively Precious Moments character, so he added a band of lace to the bottom of her skirt and around her sleeves.

Nobody's Perfect

His Love Will Shine On You

Faith Takes The Plunge

Bless Those Who Serve Their Country

Sam wasn't satisfied with the original version of a piece he designed to commemorate the tenth anniversary of Thc Precious Moments Collectors' Club in 1990. Sam thought the little fellow in the race car looked rather plain, so he designed a checkered flag and a front license plate for the car to be included in the revised version.

There have also been instances when Sam has deleted, rather than added, details. The prototype for *Bless Those Who Serve Their Country* showed a soldier carrying two bags. Because Sam wanted this piece to be less expensive, and therefore available to many people, he changed it to a single suitcase. Sam's artistry is always linked with his sensitivity toward all the people who collect and treasure Precious Moments.

10 Years And Still Going Strong

have bangs. Could you please give a Precious Moment a cowlick?

Thank you
Katelyn Elizabeth H Godfrey

Although Sam has touched many hearts, he will be the first to admit that many hearts have touched his as well. One of the most delightful of these stories came from a little girl in California named Katie Beth Godfrey. Her wistful tale became the inspiration for a new Precious Moments figurine.

Katie wrote a letter to Sam explaining that unlike all the Precious Moments children she had seen, she didn't have bangs; she had a cowlick instead. Wouldn't Sam make a Precious Moments figurine with a cowlick?

Above: *Young Katie Beth Godfrey, who asked Sam for a Precious Moments figurine with a cowlick "like hers."*
Right: *Faxes and letters between Sam and Fujioka-san discussing how to perfect Katie's figurine.*

PEARL ORIGINAL
FAX:( ) TEL:( )

SEP. 11, 1992

TO: MR. SAMUEL J. BUTCHER FROM: HISASHI SHIBUKAWA

DEAR SIR;

THIS IS TO CONFIRM MY TELEPHONE CONVERSATION WITH NIKI YESTERDAY.
REGARDING TO THE FIGURINE FOR KATIE, THE GIRL WITH COWLICK, PLEASE FIND ATTACHED SKETCH THAT WE RECEIVED.
WE HAVE STARTED WORKING ON THIS PIECE. THE TIME OF COMPLETION WE ESTIMATE IS THE MIDDLE OF NOVEMBER.
WE WILL ADVISE YOU WHEN IT IS DONE & ASK YOU WHERE WE CAN SEND OR BRING IT TO YOU.

SINCERELY YOURS

HISASHI SHIBUKAWA

TO: MR FUJIOKA
FROM: SAM BUTCHER
REGARDING: MEETING IN BANGKOK, THAILAND

MR BUTCHER WILL BE LEAVING FOR BANGKOK ON THE 15th OF FEBRUARY. HE WOULD LIKE TO MEET WITH YOU AT THE SHANG-RILA HOTEL ON THE 16th OF FEBRUARY, THURSDAY. IF THAT FITS IN YOUR SCHEDULE.

PLEASE BRING THE CLAY MOLD OF THE "PRETTY AS A PICTURE" FIGURINE AS WELL AS THE FINAL/CORRECTED FIGURINE.

IF THE SCHEDULE IS OKAY, PLEASE LET US KNOW.

THANK YOU

PEARL ORIGINAL
FAX:( ) TEL:( )

TO: MR. SAMUEL J. BUTCHER FROM: HISASHI SHIBUKAWA Mar 29, 1993
ATTN: NIKKI

DEAR MR. BUTCHER AND NIKKI;

WE HAVE SENT THE ALL CORRESPONDENCE REGARDING TO THE KATIE PROJECT TO CARTHAGE, MO. TODAY VIA FEDERAL EXPRESS.
PLEASE CONFIRM UPON RECEIPT.

SINCERELY YOURS,
HISASHI

lift frame up to show more of head. aprox.. 3/8"

Thank you
SamB

Dear Mr. Hishashi,

Thank You for sending the figurine of Katie. It is adorable and I know that she will love it. The only thing I ask is that the frame be raised 3/8 of an inch up while leaving the hands as they were so that we can see Kati's head.

I will be in Bangkok sometime during the middle of february. Just keep the figurine with you. Either we could meet in the airport at Narita or in Bangkok, whatever is best for you.

Please see the sketch above.

Sam got busy. He responded to Katie's letter, then drew the design for *You're As Pretty As A Picture,* and sent it to Fujioka-san with explicit instructions to be sure to include a cowlick on this little porcelain figurine.

The first prototype covered up too much of the girl's face—and her cowlick—so Sam raised the frame to show more of her lovely features.

After the corrections were made, Sam flew from Nagoya to Los Angeles, where he presented Katie with her very own figurine, *You're As Pretty As A Picture.*

You're As Pretty As A Picture

Left: Sam presenting You're As Pretty As A Picture *— with a cowlick — to a beaming Katie Beth at a special dinner he hosted in her honor in Los Angeles.*

Sam welcomes Dr. Sugar to Sugar Town.

In 1992, Sam created the first pieces of Sugar Town,™ a porcelain bisque re-creation of life in a small town. It is populated by many of the people who have been important in Sam's life: Sam's grandfather is depicted as the preacher, the carolers are his Aunt Dorothy, Aunt Ruth, and his grandson, Philip. Sam himself is the young boy painting the sign that reads "Sugar Town."

Inspiration for this porcelain village came from the stories about his own birth. On December 31, 1938, his parents were celebrating New Year's Eve when Sam decided to arrive early. The family physician, Dr. Sam Sugar, paid a house call and Samuel John Butcher was born at 12:15 a.m. on New Year's Day 1939.

Dr. Sam Sugar is everyone's idea of a real family doctor.

Years later Dr. Sugar wrote to Sam: "The events of your birth will always be indelibly sketched in my mind. You were my one and only New Year's baby . . . It is gratifying to know one of my babies reached such prominence. May the good Lord be with you."

"*Sugar Town* is both dear and personal to me," says Sam, "As the town grows, collectors can relive with me the people and events that changed my life, and relate them to events in their own lives."

The good Dr. Sugar's New Year's Day delivery of baby Sam Butcher in 1939 was the inspiration behind the Precious Moments Sugar Town *village.*

Dr. Sugar
The Doctor is Out
Happy New Year
Sugar
Christmas Puppies FREE

Moments of Inspiration

Tracie Hilgert

Tracie Hilgert is a busy young woman. In addition to attending school full-time and working a forty-hour week in the entertainment department at Walt Disney World, Tracie also volunteers at a school for learning-disabled children and finds time to participate in many Precious Moments fund-raisers dressed as a costumed character. Tracie carries it all off with uncommon grace.

"The first Precious Moments piece I bought was This Day Has Been Made In Heaven, *for my sister's first communion. Then I started collecting for myself.*

"Onward Christian Soldiers *is my favorite piece. There is so much going on in my life that sometimes I feel just like that little boy holding the shield in front of him. It's perfect because he looks like he's having a rough day but he keeps on going. Sometimes when I'm really busy or frustrated he gives me the inspiration I need to make it through another day."*

Onward Christian Soldiers

Sam's belief in the Lord shines through every detail of each Precious Moments figurine. His faith is the heart of the collection and the spirit that has made the figurines so much more than charming knick-knacks.

Precious Moments subjects offer words of hope and encouragement to thousands of collectors; their messages have helped many people reaffirm their faith, even in troubled times. As one collector said, "We are reminded constantly of Bible verses that we need to fit into our daily lives as we look upon these precious figurines."

Whether displayed in fancy curio cabinets or simply sitting on a kitchen shelf, the figurines become part of our lives, and their messages words to live by.

Trust In The Lord is a piece that has guided and uplifted many people. Sam created this figurine for a friend, Mark, who was going to school to become a missionary pilot. Mark had become discouraged and uncertain about his future. Sam drew the little angel to inspire him.

Sam's family Bible is one of his most cherished possessions.

Trust In The Lord

There were times in Sam's own life when his faith led him forward in spite of great difficulties. At the beginning of his career, the Child Evangelism Fellowship had offered him a job in the shipping department, promising to move him into the art department as soon as there was an opening.

So Sam and Katie sold just about everything they had, including their car, and Katie's father drove them to Grand Rapids, Michigan in his pickup. Sam said, "Most of our friends thought we were going off the deep end, but we knew this was the Lord's will and we were willing to take that step by faith."

The memory of his early struggles inspired Sam to create *Walking By Faith.*

Walking By Faith

The Joy Of The Lord Is My Strength has helped Lauri Boysen survive many trying days. As a mother of triplets, she said nothing could have prepared her for the thirty-four bottles and twenty-eight diapers her babies would use every day.

"When I saw this figurine I knew it was perfect, for it truly represented what was happening in our home. It reminds me of the source of our blessings and the knowledge that we are given only what we can handle."

"Except for the Lord," Sam Butcher says, "I work alone. The Lord guides my hand as well as my heart and new Precious Moments drawings emerge, along with an appropriate text."

Sam's son-in-law, Steve, inspired him to create *In His Time*. Steve had shared with Sam his dream of being a writer. Although he hoped for quick success, Steve was willing to wait patiently, knowing that his time would come.

In His Time

"One day while Steve was working in the garden, I visualized a little boy patiently waiting for a tiny seed to grow. In my thoughts, the seed became a symbol of Steve's faith and his patience as he waited for it to protrude from the ground."

— Sam Butcher

"So many wonder why it takes so long for things to work out in our lives. I have often felt the same way myself. But I know by faith that in God's time and in His own special way, He will bring it to pass even as He promised."

Norma Branham wrote, "One of my favorite pieces is *In His Time*. I have a fault of becoming anxious and each time I walk by that cabinet, I see that little figurine and am reminded to wait upon the Lord and everything will be all right."

I Believe In Miracles

I Believe In Miracles, which has served as a commemorative piece for the Make-A-Wish Foundation of America, was created by Sam as an emblem of his everlasting faith.

When Bill Biel began gradually losing his eyesight, doctors told him that he might become totally blind. Sam and Bill, along with other friends and family, began to pray, and miraculously, Bill's eyes healed and his eyesight returned. Sam said, "This figurine is testimony to the power of a living God."

"In 1983, I was a wife and a mother of three boys with a job I liked, a wonderful family, good friends, and a brain tumor," wrote one brave young woman. Luckily, the tumor was benign, but several years later, two more tumors were found, and she fell apart. Then, a good friend gave her the figurine *I Believe In Miracles*.

"It was the perfect gift. Surgery was successful, thanks to God, my doctor, and the prayers of my family and my friends. Miracles do indeed happen."

Moments of Love

Angie and Kathy Birchmeir

Kathy Birchmeir has been deaf since birth, but this doesn't dampen the joy in the heart and smile of this Chesaning, Michigan mother and housewife; her nine-year-old daughter, Angie, is her special link to the world of the hearing.

"I'm my mother's ears and voice!" explains Angie enthusiastically. "I've been signing for her since I was about four. My dad is hearing-impaired, too.

"I love knowing sign language. It's a special way to talk to people. All my friends want to learn because they like my mom and want to talk to her.

"My mom and I have a really special relationship and we like a lot of the same things. We both love Precious Moments and belong to two collectors' clubs. Last year my Aunt Laurie gave us A Universal Love. *It's our favorite piece.*

"When I grow up I want to work with deaf people or maybe even write a book about how hard it is to be deaf."

A Universal Love

Words of love are all around us and never-ending. Countless songs and poems have been inspired by love, and hundreds of movies and plays have been made celebrating it. But these fleeting words and pictures linger only in the mind; sometimes we want a more lasting reminder of those special times when someone says, "I love you."

Precious Moments figurines express love in every imaginable way. From the most romantic of all situations—when a suitor "pops the question"—to those quiet, magical moments when ordinary days are made extraordinary by a simple declaration of love, there's a Precious Moments figurine that captures just the right expression of this most powerful emotion.

No one understands this better than the mothers of children born with serious medical complications. Though the family has suffered great heartache, one mother with a chronically ill young son writes, "Every time I hold the figurine of the mother and child, I realize again that *Love Is The Best Gift Of All.*"

Love Is The Best Gift Of All

"I have found that love, above all else, seems to be the key to making the world a better place. Nowhere is love more evident than in the eyes and hearts of children."

—Sam Butcher

The figurines that illustrate engagements and weddings are enormously popular. Enesco receives hundreds of letters every year that describe how collectors have given and received their figurines in myriad romantic ways.

"I will always remember May 15, 1988," writes one young bride. "It was the day Tim proposed to me. He took me to dinner and after we'd finished, the waitress came to our table with a silver platter. On the platter was the Precious Moments figurine, *With This Ring I. . .*, and two glasses of champagne."

Another young man carefully selected the *Wishing You A Perfect Choice* figurine to give his girlfriend when he proposed. Like the boy in the figurine, he made a poster saying "Please check, Yes or No." He wrote, "The ring sparkled on her finger and the figurine seemed to smile as she tearfully checked the box that said 'Yes.'"

Many people began their collection with *The Lord Bless You And Keep You*. Some brides can't stop with just this one figurine. "Our white and pink wedding cake consisted of six sections. Each section was connected to the next with a mini-staircase that showcased Precious Moments figurines," wrote one beaming bride.

The Lord Bless You And Keep You *tops thousands of wedding cakes each year.*

With This Ring I. . .

Wishing You A Perfect Choice

Friends Never Drift Apart

Something's Missing When You're Not Around

Although some people may argue that "absence makes the heart grow fonder," most of us are fairly miserable when separated from friends and family. However, the love that people share can build bridges that span time and great distances.

A young bride from Colorado, away from her family for the first time, writes, "I was living with my husband and his family after mine moved away. It was my nineteenth birthday and I was feeling kind of lonely. When the mail came there was a package for me from my family. I opened it and found the Precious Moments figurine, *Something's Missing When You're Not Around.* I cried when I saw it. She was so cute and the saying couldn't have been better."

Yvonne and her friend, Ricky, had been close since nursery school. When Ricky left to go to the University of Massachusetts, he and Yvonne had a long talk and promised each other that they would never let distance affect their friendship. Then Ricky gave her *Friends Never Drift Apart.* "I know no matter how far from each other we are," says Yvonne, "he will always be in my heart."

Family love is like no other; its strength is unlimited and invincible. Sam has created numerous figurines that depict the love of a mother, father, sister, or brother. Often inspired by his own family members, Sam has made figurines based on all of his children, as well as his sister Dawn (*Dawn's Early Light*), his brother Ray (*God's Ray Of Mercy*), his grandmother Ethel (*Grandma's Prayer*), and his mother (*I'm Sending You A White Christmas*). Sam has also created an entire sub-collection, *Sammy's Circus*, starring his many beloved grandchildren.

"I feel that *Love Covers All* was created especially for me," writes Stacey Short. Stacey grew up watching her grandmother quilt and always wanted to try it herself. As her grandmother grew older, her eyesight began to fail until she could no longer make her beloved quilts, although she could still teach Stacey. After her grandmother died, Stacey wrote, "I miss the special times we shared sewing together, but thanks to Sam, this figurine brings back those cherished memories."

Love Covers All

"My Grandma Ethel will always have a special place in my heart because I still seem to hear her say, 'Sammy, Grandma prays for you.' I can still feel her protection on my frequent trips across the sea. Although death has closed her eyes and silenced her faithful prayers, my Grandma's words live on."

— Sam Butcher

Sam's neighbor, Bill Webb (shown with his granddaughter). Bill's love of building birdhomes was an inspiration to Sam.

Sam was inspired to create the 1992 Precious Moments Members Only figurine, *Only Love Can Make A Home*, by memories of a friend and neighbor, Mr. Webb. Bill Webb and his granddaughter used to walk through the hills close to Sam's home and find a favorite fishing hole, or just sit and enjoy nature.

"I learned a lot about being a grandpa and about helping God's creatures through the special friendship of my neighbor, Mr. Webb," Sam recalls.

"Mr. Webb loved blue birds. He would feed them and he would lovingly build houses for them. Some people build birdhouses . . . Mr. Webb built birdhomes. He built love into every one, and the birds flocked to live in them every spring."

Today Mr. Webb's birdhomes can be found all over the Chapel grounds in Carthage, Missouri.

The first prototype of Only Love Can Make A Home *had bright yellow birds. When Sam saw it, he insisted the birds be painted blue in honor of his old friend.*

The tranquil Secret Garden is one of Sam's favorite spots on the Chapel grounds.

"As a grandpa, I try to find experiences to share with my beautiful grandchildren that will bring joy and memories to treasure throughout our lives. Sharing the pleasures of nature is one of our favorite pastimes."

—Sam Butcher

The Secondary Market

In the world of collectibles, products may create so much demand that a "secondary market" is born. Certain sought-after pieces, including those no longer in production because they've been retired (the mold has been broken and the figurines will never again be made) or suspended (not currently being produced), limited editions, Members Only figurines such as *Only Love Can Make A Home*, and pieces with older year marks may go up in value over their original issue price. Many Precious Moments figurines are highly sought after, and their secondary market prices reflect collector demand. It's not unheard of for pieces that once sold for under twenty dollars to sell for hundreds of dollars or more on the secondary market—at Swap 'N Sells, through private sales, or through retailers who specialize in the pieces. Collectors say searching for that hard-to-find item is all part of the fun of collecting. And every collector dreams of finding a rare piece that is tucked away in a little country store or down the street at a neighbor's tag sale.

Moments of Friendship

Irene Ng and Donna Pon

Irene and Donna have been friends for many years. Their husbands are also close friends and the two families live near one another in Edison, New Jersey. It was after they discovered Precious Moments together, though, that these two women really cemented their friendship.

"Several years ago my mother gave me Make A Joyful Noise,*" Irene said, "and the floodgates were opened. Donna went to her first Precious Moments event by herself, but she was so enthusiastic about it we decided to go to the next one together.*

"About two years ago we joined a local club together, and now our husbands and kids go to some of the fund-raising events. The best part about collecting together is that we know what the other one wants, so we can tell our husbands or family what to get. We drop hints for each other.

"Even though we share a lot of the same interests, collecting Precious Moments is one of the best things we do together."

Make A Joyful Noise

To My Forever Friend

We Need A Good Friend Through The Ruff Times

The moments shared between friends are moments to be cherished for a lifetime. Judging by the number of Precious Moments dedicated to this subject, it's clear that Sam Butcher is a firm believer in friends.

The very first figurine Sam created, *Love One Another,* shows a little boy and girl sitting on a tree stump together. They look as if they've been sharing secrets and dreams—the glue that holds friends together.

Friends are people who stick by you through the good times and the bad. Sam certainly had this in mind when he created *We Need A Good Friend Through The Ruff Times.* One collector wrote, "I wanted to find a Precious Moments figurine for my collection that said it all about my friend, John. John has been there for me since my Dad passed away a year ago. He has become an extended part of my family as another 'big brother.' I can always count on John to lend a hand and to listen when I need to talk, even when he might be busy. Each time I look at that figurine in my curio, a smile comes to my face as I remember my big brother, John, whom I know I can count on through the good times and the 'ruff times.'"

Sometimes a Precious Moments figurine helps celebrate a new friendship while other times it serves to honor an old one. A new collector writes, "I had never heard of Precious Moments before. One day I was doing volunteer work at my son's school, and the teacher showed me a book of the Precious Moments Christmas. Right away I fell in love with them. At the end of the year she bought me a special gift, *To My Forever Friend*. I was almost in tears. She made me feel like someone special. We are real good friends and she makes me feel like one of her family members."

Christine, Maryann, and Diane were best friends for many years. When Christine planned to move to England, her companions were sad but decided to take Diane's infant daughter to her first Precious Moments event before Christine left. Here they bought her *Good Friends Are Forever*. Christine wrote to say that "no matter how many miles away, our friendship will never die out. We thank you for allowing us to remember all our Precious Moments together."

Good Friends Are Forever

Friendship Hits The Spot

That's What Friends Are For

It's almost uncanny how so many Precious Moments illustrate our own personal experiences and relationships; often, they seem to replicate our closest friendships.

"Dee and I may have been born sisters but we became best friends," writes Tammy from Texas. "I don't think Sam could have created a more personal figurine if he would have asked me himself. *Friendship Hits The Spot* had to be mine because it's a porcelain memory of my best friend, Dee, and I waking up early to play tea party when we were little. When people ask why this figurine is out in front of the others in my collection, I can answer that no matter how many friends I make through the years, Dee will always stand out in front."

Sandra wrote from Tennessee to say that she and her friend, Debbie, helped each other through some trying times. When Sandra moved a thousand miles away, Debbie gave her *That's What Friends Are For.*

"The two girls holding and comforting each other truly reflect how Debbie and I managed to survive our burdens through our love and support for each other."

When Sam's good friend, Jean Besett, was ill with cancer, he visited her in the hospital and tried to find words to cheer her up and ease her pain.

She squeezed his hand and whispered, "Don't worry, I'm not afraid. He stands beside me." Inspired by Jean's unflinching courage, Sam created a figurine especially for her.

Sam presented Jean with the figurine, *He Stands Beside Me,* before her death on June 20, 1990.

As a tribute to Jean's memory, a duplicate of this figurine is on display at the Precious Moments Chapel in Carthage, Missouri.

Friday

The Carthage Press

28¢ + 2¢ tax Total 30¢

Volume 106 Number 13

June 8, 1990

Southwest Missouri's Oldest Daily Newspaper

Carthage woman inspires Butcher

By NANCY PRATER
Carthage Press Lifestyles Editor

A Carthage woman who is seriously ill with cancer has provided the latest inspiration for a figurine by Precious Moments creator Sam Butcher. The artist credits Jean Besett, now a patient at McCune-Brooks Hospital, with inspiring him to continue with his dream of building the now famous chapel.

Cutting down a process that normally takes about two years, Butcher was able to take his figurine from his Carthage drawing board to the finished porcelain figurine made in Indonesia a few days later.

Butcher says he then was able to deliver the finished product to his friend at her hospital bed just a day before her condition worsened. She reportedly is no longer able to communicate verbally with those around her.

Butcher began his friendship with Mrs. Besett three years ago when she was operating The Christian Bookstore at 321 Airport Drive. At this time, facing the pressures of finishing the chapel, he would find himself going to the bookstore seeking encouragement through his conversations with Mrs. Besett.

"Basically I'm a loner and I had nobody to share my feelings with," he relates. "I would get discouraged and go to this little Christian bookstore. Jean would always find a book to encourage me. I was always touched by her insight and sensitivity."

JEAN BESETT
'Her message is here'

"I can remember going into the gift shop and she would be so sweet," he said.

One day recently Butcher came in for a talk only to learn she was ill and in the hospital. Wishing to give his friend encouragement, he and his son, Jon, drove over to visit her.

From her hospital bed Mrs. Besett told Butcher of her pain, but also told him, "I know that the Lord is beside me and I'm not afraid."

"I felt so foolish," he says, "Here I had come over to minister to her and she ended up ministering to me."

Touched and inspired by her ministry, Butcher immediately made reservations to fly to Indonesia, where one of the Precious Moments figurine factories is located. Completing his sketches in Carthage, he spent the plane flight painting his sketches. Once in Indonesia, he and a carver worked all night and half of the following day sculpting his creation. The porcelain figure was completed and approved by master [illegible] Yashuhei Fujioka about a [illegible]

Annexation, [illegible]

Jean Besett's courage and faith during her battle with cancer inspired Sam to create the figurine He Stands Beside Me.

Moments of Celebration

Bill Heyden

Bill Heyden is a carpenter and construction worker from the greater Chicago area. Although Bill's strong, skilled hands look as if they could move mountains, he is a gentle, happy man whose passion is collecting Precious Moments figurines.

"My wife and I celebrate every special occasion by buying a new Precious Moments figurine. We enjoy collecting together, especially when we're traveling. Our first piece was given to us for our twenty-fifth wedding anniversary. After that we were off and running.

"Several years ago my youngest son was getting married and when we were ready to leave for the church ceremony, he couldn't find the rings anywhere. Finally he looked behind the sofa, and there was our little Pomeranian dog, Ginger, with the ring box in her mouth. Ever since then our favorite piece has been With This Ring I . . ."

With This Ring I . . .

A typically happy event becomes a festive celebration when you reach out and share the occasion with others. Some celebrations, such as birthdays, graduations, weddings, births, and anniversaries, are a part of all our lives. Other milestones—a new job, a raise, reaching an important goal— are less predictable but equally exciting. Sam Butcher has created a piece to capture the joy of each and every celebration.

Sam's figurines have special meaning for older collectors, who use them to jog their memories and to relive the festive occasions of the past. Carolyn Keith of Akron, Ohio writes, "As we get older, the months and years of life go by so fast. When you see the figurines Sam has made, it makes you feel like you have your youth again. You may have forgotten, but Precious Moments figurines help you remember your younger days. You think about those memories which made you happy and gave you pleasure."

"These little people with their teardrop eyes have given me a renewed interest in life. Every time I see a new one I say, 'I just gotta have it,' " wrote seventy-one-year-old Margaret Miller.

Many Moons In Same Canoe, Blessum You

Weddings and anniversaries are such fun to celebrate! And the careful selection of a meaningful gift makes them even more unforgettable.

Frank Yesh gave his wife Marian *Many Moons In Same Canoe, Blessum You* for their thirty-fourth anniversary. Some time before this, Frank had suffered a severe heart attack. "This figurine serves to remind me just how easily the canoe of life can be tipped," writes Marian, "and how we need to take the time to appreciate our loved ones while we can."

Margaret and Bill Wasmuth spent their twenty-sixth anniversary working on renovating their daughter's first home, cleaning, painting, and installing a new floor. To celebrate, Bill gave Margaret *Thumb Body Loves You*. "Renovating was not a first choice for an anniversary," Margaret admits, "but as we worked together we were able to give a gift of love to our children. We'll remember this anniversary each time we see this figurine."

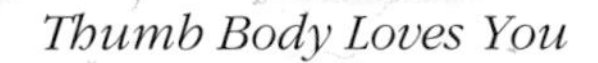

Thumb Body Loves You

Sometimes people have to work very hard before they are able to celebrate. Regina Cajigas wrote that she had always dreamed of going to college but there were so many bills to pay at home, she had to go to work to help support her family. Finally, she saved enough money to enroll.

"It took a long time but I finally graduated," Regina recalls. "Upon graduation, a friend gave me *The Lord Bless You And Keep You*, and I began to cry. Now every time I look at the figurine, I am reminded that even though life is a struggle, the Lord is there to bless and keep me and there is always a way as long as I keep trying."

Louise Lucci struggled to maintain her grades in college while she worked part-time. During her last semester, a teacher told her that if she did not make an "A" on the exam, she would not graduate. Louise's father called her to say, "All I can ask of you is to try your best and that is all you can ask of yourself."

Louise aced the exam, and that very night her father presented her with *Seek And Ye Shall Find*. "Now every time I feel like life is getting the best of me," wrote Louise, "I look at that special Precious Moments figurine and know that with my family and the Lord on my side I can continue to face life's challenges and cherish all the wonderful times ahead."

The Lord Bless You And Keep You

Seek And Ye Shall Find

The joy Sam and Katie's adopted daughter, Heather, brought them inspired Sam to create God Bless The Day We Found You.

Although every new life is filled with joy and promise, babies come in all shapes and sizes, and arrive in many different ways. Sam's own daughter, Heather, was adopted shortly before her fifth birthday. Heather was living in a foster home but spending a lot of time with the Butchers, who were then struggling to make ends meet. They knew in their hearts that Heather belonged with them, and their love for this child overcame all obstacles. Inspired by his love for Heather, Sam created *God Bless The Day We Found You* to recognize and celebrate the special love that comes with an adopted child.

The parents of two adopted children write, "It's so seldom that we adoptive parents find tokens of our unique kind of love."

One couple adopted a six-month-old baby from Romania. "Today we look at our son and can't believe how blessed we are to have him in our lives," they write. "Sam Butcher must have had the same inspiration to create such a beautiful figurine. Thank you for capturing our feelings with this beautiful keepsake."

Moments of Sympathy

Alice Koss

Alice Koss's eyes light up when she talks about her Precious Moments figurines. Homemaker, mother, grandmother, and community volunteer, Alice is also an enthusiastic and supportive member of several chapters of the Precious Moments Collectors' Club.

"My husband gave me my first Precious Moments piece, a little bear that I love dearly. Through the years, he gave me several figurines, Thee I Love *and* Love One Another, *which are two of my favorites.*

"My husband never had a chance to collect many of the Precious Moments figurines, but he did collect antiques and different kinds of barbed wire. I know he'd be happy that I've kept up my own collection and I think of him whenever I add a new piece.

"When he passed away several years ago, I got Hello, Lord, It's Me Again*— the Enesco Precious Moments Charter Members Only figurine. It's my favorite piece now! The little boy holding the phone, and all the figurines he gave me remind me of the happy times we had together."*

Hello, Lord, It's Me Again

When tragedy strikes, it seems as if the world is going to crumble around us. But, as Sam's figurine of the little nurse and her clock gently reminds us, time heals all wounds.

"We don't always see what a big part of our lives a person is until that person is gone. Last July we lost a very special person in my family, my Uncle Bob. Last Christmas was the first holiday without him. It was the hardest day I could ever remember until I opened a gift from my special godson, Justin. It was the Precious Moments *Time Heals*. Whenever I see it, I remember how much Uncle Bob loved us and how much he was loved," wrote one collector.

Soon after her new baby was baptized, one collector's father was diagnosed with terminal cancer. She was devastated and her father tried to make her feel better by telling her that "time heals." Three months after her father's death, she began training to become a licensed practical nurse. Just before she graduated, her mother gave her the figurine *Time Heals*. She wrote, "It was a most precious moment. I remembered again those words my father had said: time heals."

No Tears Past The Gate

Time Heals

Precious Moments' messages have reached across oceans and continents to comfort those in need.

Sam has spent a great deal of time in the Philippines working in the ministry. He often speaks in churches and Bible schools. Several years ago, his assistant came to him and confided that his sister was dying. Sam, wanting to offer a voice of sympathy and comfort to this man who had worked with him so tirelessly, painted *No Tears Past The Gate*. It is a living reminder of Psalm 30:5: "Weeping may endure for a night, but joy comes in the morning."

Laurene Klas wrote to say that twenty-nine years ago, she gave birth to a sweet baby girl who, tragically, died exactly nine months later.

"This little girl cried so much and we didn't know why until four days before she died. Linda Laura was diagnosed with leukemia. My four living children gave me *No Tears Past The Gate* for Christmas. I feel our baby was finally put to rest in our earthly lives. I cry when I look at the figurine, as I know she is finally smiling."

Moments of Encouragement

Nadine and Chuck Breen

Nadine and Chuck Breen have filled their Lynchburg, Virginia house with Precious Moments figurines. Chuck works as a salesman, and Nadine teaches music at a neighborhood Christian school. Together, they are the devoted parents of Kyle, twelve, and Brittany, nine.

"My first piece, Make A Joyful Noise*, couldn't have been more appropriate, since I teach music," Nadine says. "My aunt gave it to me when I graduated from college, and it's still one of my favorites.*

"Another one of my favorites is Love Lifted Me*, which shows the little boy and girl on the see-saw. Chuck gave it to me one day when I was all discouraged about my work.*

"It's hard sometimes to have to teach every day, but his love and encouragement help a lot. He really keeps me 'up' about my job, so this figurine seemed to be made just for us."

Love Lifted Me

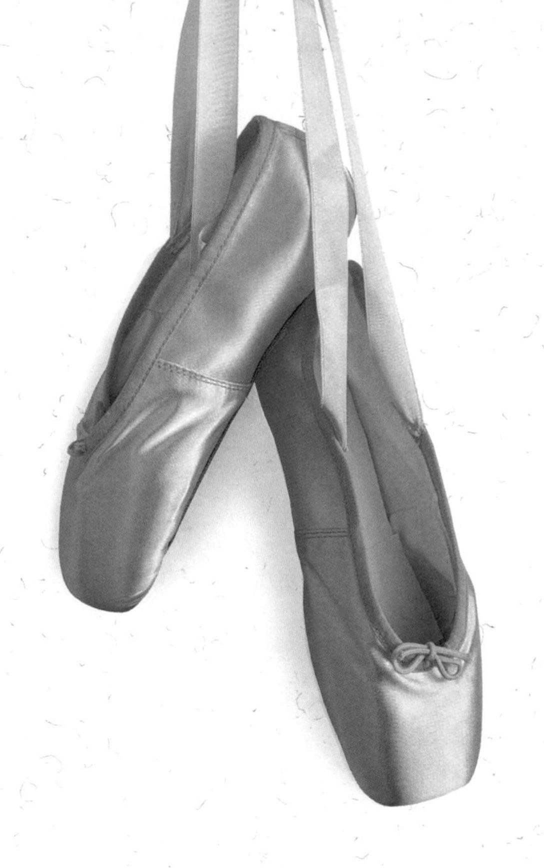

There are ups and downs in everyone's life—times when everything goes along smoothly, and other times when it seems we're faced with insurmountable obstacles.

Precious Moments figurines have become wonderful tokens of support for many people. These wide-eyed children seem to lend a helping hand and a warm smile whenever and wherever somebody needs a boost.

Many young collectors have been guided through their tough times by Sam's messages of encouragement. Christina Garden, who had taken ballet lessons for twelve years, wrote about the anticipation and anxiety she experienced waiting to get her first pointe shoes.

"When I finally got them, I was scared. I had heard of so many girls who hurt their ankles and couldn't dance again. I didn't want that to happen to me. Right after I went to the store and got my pointe shoes, my Mom surprised me with *Lord, Keep Me On My Toes*. That wasn't my very first Precious Moment, but it was my own very greatest moment, and that figurine became my favorite. And from that moment on I wasn't as scared as much as I was before."

Lord, Keep Me On My Toes

Sometimes it's difficult to remember that ultimately everything happens for a reason. A favorite figurine in the collection, *The Lord Giveth, And The Lord Taketh Away*, is a wonderful reminder of this.

Sam's inspiration was something that took place in his own household. Arriving home from the Philippines one day, he walked into a house full of feathers, tears, and one very happy cat. Katie stood by an empty bird cage, where the cat was licking her paws.

Everyone was sad to lose the bird, but Sam was so inspired he grabbed pencil and paper and began sketching the first drawings for this figurine.

The inspiration for the 1992 Members Only figurine, *Sowing The Seeds Of Love*, came from Sam's youngest daughter, Heather. In Sam's words, "She has always loved to make things grow."

"One summer day, as I was walking through the chapel grounds in Carthage, I saw Heather. She was covered from head to toe in dirt. When she looked up at me with her big, bright eyes and a proud smile, she said, 'Isn't it beautiful, Dad?'

"I was a little surprised until I realized that she was talking about a new flower that had just come up. I was deeply touched to see that she was looking past the dirt to see the beauty underneath."

The Lord Giveth, And The Lord Taketh Away

Sowing The Seeds Of Love

One woman wrote that after ten years of marriage, she and her husband were struggling in their relationship. "One day I went to the mall to get away from the anger I felt at home. I was walking around and saw the Precious Moments figurine, *Be Not Weary In Well Doing.* Right next to it was the bride figurine. I realized that I had been unfair. God didn't bring us together so we'd give up when things got tough."

She bought the little cleaning lady and returned home to her husband and children filled with gratitude and renewed devotion. Now, as they prepare to celebrate their seventeenth wedding anniversary, she continues to be thankful for the "little lady" who reminds her of the happiness that two people can achieve sharing their dreams, goals, and their love for a lifetime.

Bless You Two

Be Not Weary In Well Doing

Sweep All Your Worries Away

"Thank you, Sam, for seeing good in all jobs great and small and bringing us such joy," wrote Marge Lewis.

"I am a mother with three children. Once when I was exhausted from household chores, my husband handed me *Sweep All Your Worries Away.* I laughed at the all-too familiar scene. My husband said nothing but his eyes and smile said it all."

Sam was once asked if there was a specific incident that had inspired the figurine *Help, Lord, I'm In A Spot.* He said, "Many years ago, I was doing a series of out-of-town TV shows and worked in my hotel room, a nice big room with a bright green rug. In my haste to meet the deadline, I spilled a bottle of black ink. Being 'on the spot,' literally, I had to do something to cover up my 'sin,' so I mixed up some matching green paint and 'touched up' the carpet. You could hardly tell the difference . . . 'til the paint dried and got harder than cement!"

Help, Lord, I'm In A Spot

Small Moments

Jackie, Ricky, and Ashley Hanks

Precious Moments collectors Jackie and Ricky Hanks were born and raised in the heart of Texas. Their fourteen-year-old daughter, Ashley, a cheerleader at her LaPorte, Texas school, loves to collect with them, making it a family hobby. Though they collect dolls and other figurines, the Hanks say it is their Precious Moments Collection that is closest to their hearts.

"We're a family of collectaholics!" Jackie says, laughing. "It's really all Ricky's fault. When I was pregnant with Ashley, he gave me Mother Sew Dear *for Mother's Day and we've been hooked ever since. Ashley has really been a collector since before she was born.*

"When she began taking ballet lessons, we gave Ashley Lord, Keep Me On My Toes. *Now her favorite is* He Is Not Here For He Has Risen As He Said *because it reminds her of her church activities.*

"I don't think that I would be as avid a collector just for myself, but I love to collect as a family. The pieces are reminders of all the things we have shared together."

Mother Sew Dear

Moments of Hope for the World

Jean Hunter

Jean Hunter, an analytical chemist from Staten Island, New York, radiates love for her family, her job, and her Precious Moments figurine collection.

"I always loved the figurines, but it was the people that really made Precious Moments special. I experienced their loving, caring, and sharing even before I knew that this was their motto. I've never met a group of people who accepted me and loved me so much for who I am.

"I've met many different kinds of collectors from all faiths and backgrounds, and we all respect Sam's message of loving your fellow man. There seems to be a divine spirit that binds us all together.

"I just purchased the first "Good Samaritan" figurine. I can't tell you how many prayers I've said for people I don't even know, but I like the idea of all of us pulling together to help those in need."

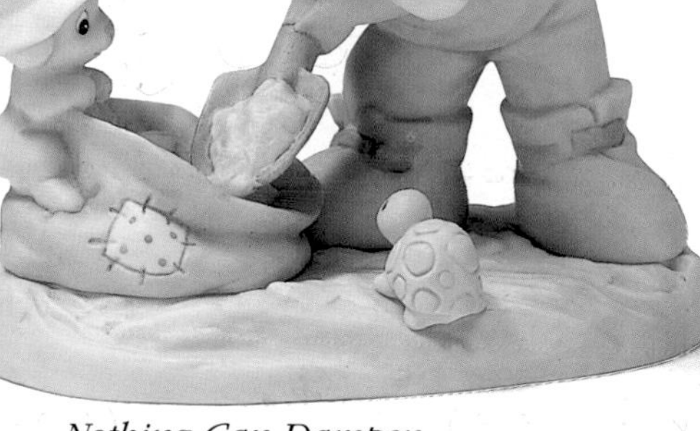

Nothing Can Dampen The Spirit Of Caring

Precious Moments figurines have reached thousands of collectors throughout the world and their messages of faith and love have been heard by people of all races and nationalities.

In recognition of the growth of a world community, and the increased need for global understanding, Enesco has issued several figurines that express Sam's hopes for universal peace and a healthy environment for all. Some of the figurines, such as *Money Isn't The Only Green Thing Worth Saving*, reflect Sam's belief in preserving our natural resources. This is also a wonderful example of his sense of humor and his love of puns and wordplay.

Sam's ministry has grown with the times. As new concerns touch our lives, Sam's little messengers continue to give us support, encouragement, and hope for the future, no matter what obstacles we encounter.

Money Isn't The Only Green Thing Worth Saving

Perfect Harmony

Vaya Con Dios,
or *GoWith God*

Perfect Harmony shows a white and a black child sitting together after trading their puppies. Sam created this piece to add his voice to those which remind us that "we are all God's children, created equal in His sight."

People of other nations bring particular delight to Sam. He has reached hundreds of people with his work in the Philippines; his daughter, Debbie, has adopted a little Filipina girl.

Sam created *Vaya Con Dios*, or *Go With God*, to reach out to those from Hispanic cultures with the universal language of Precious Moments.

One collector from Mexico wrote, "I do not know the English language. I had to ask my children to write this letter. I am a mature woman with ten children and thirteen grandchildren. I have devoted my life to them. Now, near the end, I finally had the joy of being able to travel to the United States. That was when I became a Precious Moments fan, or better, a lover.

"We are far away, but it is just the distance, because we are close in feelings. Many thanks to you all."

Reflecting on this figurine and its very special message, Sam said, "Every time I see it, I'm reminded that I can turn to Him with my problems because He is the answer."

Jesus Is The Answer

Sam Butcher has drawn thousands of familiar Precious Moments figures. Only one, *Jesus Is The Answer*, was ever framed and hung in his home. Sam created this as a tribute to world peace and freedom.

This figurine was brought back from suspension in 1992, in order to benefit St. Jude Children's Research Hospital and support their search for cures for catastrophic illnesses.

In response to the devastating floods that swept through the midwestern United States in 1993, Sam created a special figurine. In conjunction with this introduction Enesco established a special fund to help flood victims and others in need.

Appropriately titled *Nothing Can Dampen The Spirit Of Caring*, this figurine, the first in the "Good Samaritan" series, has been received with great enthusiasm and gratitude by the countless collectors, both old and new, whose lives have been affected by this disaster, or who simply appreciate the opportunity to help other people.

There are many unsung heroes in our world, people who give tirelessly of their time and energy to help others. Through the years, *You Have Touched So Many Hearts* has become a favorite gift that is given in recognition of such generous, selfless people.

One teacher wrote, "May 1986 was a very special time for me. I had been teaching the junior high students for twenty-five years at a local Catholic school. When I retired, a co-worker gave me this figurine. What a beautiful tribute, that others saw how I had touched so many hearts. I have looked at it so many times, and I pray for all those precious children I have touched with my own heart and example."

One remarkable couple with fifteen children of their own, including one foster daughter and one adopted son, has found time to work in Christian children's homes for more than thirty years. Robbie is called "Mama" by hundreds of children, and was twice named "Mother of the Year." Jack has also received well-deserved recognition as "Father of the Year."

On Robbie's sixty-first birthday, her family presented her with—what else—the figurine *Always Room For One More.*

You Have Touched So Many Hearts

In 1981 Sam created a figurine as a testament to the ministry which has been such an integral part of his life. *Turn Your Eyes Upon Jesus* shows a captain of a washtub ship looking through a telescope that is turned toward the heavens. This figurine is to be held off the market until after Sam's death. It will be his legacy and his last message to all those who love Precious Moments.

Turn Your Eyes Upon Jesus

Then in the quiet of the morn
beside the crystal sea
my Savior in that still small voice
began to speak to me.

My vessels are not chosen
just to glory in their fame
but they are called to magnify
and bear my precious name.

Knowing that the gifts
or any talents that they share
cannot melt a single heart
unless my blessing's there.

—Sam Butcher, 1982

The Precious Moments Community

It probably began over a pot of coffee, with two friends discussing their favorite new hobby, collecting Precious Moments figurines. Soon, they invited a third friend because she, too, loved Sam Butcher's little messengers, and then they invited a fourth and a fifth until someone began calling it a club.

It happened in Hurst, Texas and Jackson, Michigan. It happened in Bellingham, Washington and New York City and hundreds of other places all over the country. Like any good news, Precious Moments was too good not to share.

Sharing is what Precious Moments Clubs are all about—sharing thoughts about the collection, sharing ideas about new pieces, sharing information about how to care for, insure, and display the figurines.

The real sense of community developed, however, when Club members began sharing the inspirational messages of Precious Moments. The little boy and girl on the tree stump, *Love One Another*, encouraged Club members to reach out to share their love with others.

And when collectors saw *Jesus Loves Me*, they were inspired to offer their friendship and support to anyone in need.

At the request of both the collectors and the retailers who were carrying the Precious Moments line, Enesco decided to sponsor a national club. The director of the new Club, Shonnie Bilin, today Enesco's Vice President of Collectibles, was ambitious from the start and set a goal of 10,000 members for the first year. The figurine *But Love Goes On Forever* was chosen as the image for the Club logo, and "The Spirit of Loving, Caring, and Sharing," was very appropriately chosen as a motto.

Under the leadership of Shonnie Bilin, the Precious Moments Collectors' Club grew by leaps and bounds.

The figurine But Love Goes On Forever *was chosen to represent the new Collectors' Club.*

The Collectors' Clubs

Even before the Club was officially accepting members in January 1981, applications began pouring into Enesco headquarters. By the end of the year an incredible 69,000 collectors had applied for membership.

There are many reasons for the phenomenal growth of the Enesco Precious Moments Collectors' Club. Members enjoy such benefits as an annual Symbol of Membership figurine; a subscription to the quarterly magazine, the *Goodnewsletter*; receipt of the official gift registry, which identifies each Precious Moments figurine; and the opportunity to acquire exclusive Members Only figurines.

But more importantly, the Club grew because people wanted to feel that they belonged to the Precious Moments family, and were a part of the spirit of Loving, Caring, and Sharing.

The Goodnewsletter *made its debut in February of 1981. Today the* Goodnewsletter *is a beautiful full-color magazine filled with information about new introductions, retirements, suspensions, events, and Precious Moments news from across the country.*

GOODNEWSLETTER

FEBRUARY 1981 THE OFFICIAL PUBLICATION OF ENESCO'S PRECIOUS MOMENTS COLLECTORS' CLUB VOLUME 1,

CLUB PROJECTS 5000 MEMBERS IN FIRST SIX MONT

"Response has been more enthusiastic than I ever dared hope for so soon," Rosemary Davis bubbled. Our acting Club Director was surrounded by the morning mail. "Every day I try to attend to general Club business first thing because once the mail arrives, my desk is completely buried!"

"Applications are coming in from all across the country," Rosemary commented as she sorted through the pile. "Really," she confessed, "it's all I can do to keep up with it!"

Even before the Club was officially accepting members (January, this ... Precious Moments collectors ... for their first

more comment than any other is our symbol, taken from the figurine entitled "But Love Goes On Forever." It has always been one of the most popular, so it's not surprising that collectors voiced loud approval when that sculpture became the basis for the Club logo, shown below. The resemblance of the logo to the original sculpture was no accident. The creators of Precious Moments were actually involved with the adaptation of the figurine artwork for the Club!

Based on the number of collectors that have already become Charter Members, it appears likely that membership will reach the 5000 mark before the Club is even six months old! Member... quests are not only coming f... lectors nationwide, but from a... sources.

Applications are featured ... are running in the national ... All Precious Moments fi... soon have a package ins... the Collection and the Cl... to including an application. Finally, retailers who carry Precious Moments merchandise will have little stands containing a descriptive brochure and application. Be sure to pass this information along to your friends who've been wondering how they too can become Charter Members of the Club.

... A SHOESTRING

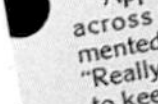

As membership in the national Club grew, many collectors became interested in forming smaller, neighborhood organizations. In response to this, guidelines were created to set standards for these local Chapters.

Each Chapter had to be sponsored by an authorized Precious Moments retailer, and each Chapter was encouraged to become involved in a philanthropy.

The response was enthusiastic and there are now over 400 Local Chapters of the Enesco Precious Moments Collectors' Club worldwide that participate in a variety of national and community service projects.

Many Chapters choose to remain small and intimate, with spur-of-the-moment get-togethers. Others have memberships numbering in the hundreds with regularly scheduled meetings and their own newsletter and club pin.

In 1985 the Precious Moments Birthday Club was formed to better fill the needs of the growing number of younger collectors. The Birthday Club offers children their own line of Members Only Birthday Club figurines and publishes a separate newsletter, the *Good News Parade.*

The combined membership of the Collectors' Club and the Birthday Club is now over 500,000; the Club continues to grow each year under the direction of Julia Kirkwood, who became the Club Director in mid-1991.

The Good News Parade *is the official publication of the Enesco Precious Moments Birthday Club.*

Many Local Chapters have created their own membership pins.

In 1991, 1992, and 1993 the National Association of Limited Edition Dealers presented the Collector Club of the Year *award to the Enesco Precious Moments Collectors' Club for "outstanding club member benefits, services, and special-event programs."*

A Perfect Display of Fifteen Happy Years commemorates the Fifteenth Anniversary of the Precious Moments Collectors' Club in 1995. Every Symbol of Membership figurine is displayed in miniature in the beautifully crafted curio cabinet.

Easter Seals®

The Easter Seal Society

Because the Enesco Corporation was enjoying such great success with the sale of the Precious Moments line, the whole Enesco family wanted to share their good fortune. In 1987 Gene Freedman began looking for a charitable organization that would help the company live out the Precious Moments motto of Loving, Caring, and Sharing.

Enesco wanted an organization that really cared about the people it served and that made a significant difference in their lives. The National Easter Seal Society, which supports programs for adults and children with disabilities, was a happy and logical choice, and in 1987 Enesco became an Easter Seal National Corporate Sponsor.

To aid in the fund-raising drive, Sam Butcher created *He Walks With Me* as the 1987 Easter Seal commemorative figurine, and Enesco employees, retailers, suppliers, vendors, and collectors joined together to raise more than $250,000 during this first year of involvement with the Easter Seal Society.

Hundreds of Enesco employees and Club members work phones from coast to coast during the annual Easter Seal Telethon.

He Walks With Me, *created in 1987, was the first Easter Seal figurine.*

Each year the entire Enesco family becomes involved in the Easter Seal fund-raising drive. Sam Butcher designs a special commemorative figurine, sales representatives donate commissions, and retailers and Collectors' Club members hold hundreds of special events, ranging from bake sales to mall walk-a-thons.

At corporate headquarters, Enesco's 700-plus employees also become involved, hosting raffles, bagel sales, golf outings, and dozens of other fund-raisers.

Gene Freedman's involvement in the Easter Seal fund-raising campaign resulted in a close friendship with the national spokesman for the Easter Seal Society, Pat Boone. Author, song-writer, public speaker, and entertainer, Pat was named the Enesco Precious Moments Collectors' Club celebrity spokesman in 1991.

Like anyone who sees Sam's Precious Moments figurines, Pat Boone fell in love with them, and he and his wife are now enthusiastic collectors.

Between 1987 and 1994 the Enesco Precious Moments family raised over $14.8 million for the National Easter Seal Society.

"I'm very proud of my friendship and association with Sam and the Precious Moments collectors and all the good folks at Enesco. I've learned firsthand the kind of individual and collective commitment that they make. It is inspiring."

— Pat Boone

Special Events

The collectors of Precious Moments are part of a large family that also includes the Enesco Corporation and over 10,000 Precious Moments authorized dealers. Special events play an important part in helping this extended family keep in touch. These events vary from holiday celebrations at local retail stores to the annual national convention for all Local Club Chapters. Participation can range from a handful of dedicated collectors to thousands of enthusiastic Club members who come to see both new figurines and old friends, and share news and ideas.

As enthusiasm for the figurines grew, both retailers and collectors requested more special events. In 1983 Phyllis Peszek joined the Enesco team as events manager. She says, "The best part of my job is meeting with members one-on-one and learning how their lives have been enhanced by collecting Precious Moments figurines. It's hardly 'work,' knowing that everywhere I go I'm going to meet and make new friends."

The bigger-than-life Precious Moments characters are always a popular attraction at special events.

The first annual Special Event figurine, You Are My Main Event, *was created in 1988.*

On October 27, 1989, Enesco sponsored the first annual national convention for Local Club Chapters. Delegates from over 400 Chapters, hailing from all fifty states and Canada, participated in this event.

For the collectors, it's a very special event indeed when they have an opportunity to meet Sam Butcher, hear him speak, and perhaps be fortunate enough to have him sign a favorite figurine.

In the summer of 1990, the Enesco Precious Moments Collectors' Club held its tenth anniversary celebration in Carthage, Missouri. Sam Butcher introduced many people who had been the inspiration for some of the most popular figurines in the collection. Included were his son, Jon (*Hello, Lord, It's Me Again*), and his friend, Chuck (*You Just Cannot Chuck A Good Friendship*).

Local, regional, and national events bring collectors together to share fun and fellowship.

Community Service

Local Chapter meetings remain the heart of Precious Moments Club participation. These get-togethers, both big and small, formal and informal, allow friendships to bloom and grow. It is also through the Local Chapters that innumerable community services are made possible.

Sam wrote to Club members to encourage them in their pursuit of Loving, Caring, and Sharing: "Your voice, and your expression of love, added to the countless voices of your fellow Club members, could be a glorious chorus."

And what a glorious song of giving it has been! Wherever they see a need, these collectors, united by the love and inspiration of Precious Moments figurines, reach out to make the lives around them a little easier, a little better, a little more full of love.

Because each Local Club chapter is involved in philanthropic endeavors, fund-raising is an essential part of the members' programs. These activities really bring out the collectors' creativity, enthusiasm, and dedication. In addition to tried-and-true projects, such as walk-a-thons and bake sales, the Precious Moments family has come up with some creative ways to raise money and gather supplies for the needy.

The "Moments to Share" and "High Hopes Precious Moments" Chapters of Rockford, Illinois work together to support the Christian Care Center and Shelter, a temporary home for battered women and children. When asked what specific needs the shelter had, the director answered, "Toilet paper!" This is a major expense for the shelter, but it is not something people often think about when making donations.

Chapter members immediately thought of the little figurine, *Lord Keep Me In Teepee Top Shape*, and decided to build a teepee of T.P. to give to the shelter. They solicited rolls of toilet paper and gave a raffle ticket for every roll donated. The person with the winning raffle ticket received the figurine. The Chapters received over 300 rolls of toilet paper, which lasted about a month at the shelter!

Local Club Chapters sponsor community activities and raise funds for everything from Canine Companions (opposite, top), which provides guide dogs for the blind, to a local shelter for battered women and children desperately in need of everyday staples such as toilet paper.

The "Friendship In A Pocket" Chapter (sponsored by the Jack Langer Pharmacy in Milwaukee), offers a wonderful example of how Local Chapter members and retailers work together to make a difference.

Throughout the year, ten percent of the profits from the sale of Precious Moments figurines at the pharmacy is donated to the Easter Seal Society.

A fund drive also goes on all year, with members of the Chapter hosting several different events to raise money. The final activity is a festive bowl-a-thon, where members are sponsored either by the pin or by the game. The Chapter, in cooperation with the Jack Langer Pharmacy, is able to donate an astounding annual contribution of over $30,000.

From bowl-a-thons and bake sales to auctions and raffles, Precious Moments collectors never run out of ideas or energy to help those in need.

Raffling off Precious Moments figurines is a very popular way to raise money. The "Love Covers All" Chapter from Newfoundland, New Jersey raffled off two large laundry baskets full of figurines. The sale of one basket benefited the Easter Seal Society and the proceeds from the other went into the Chapter treasury to fund local services and projects.

The "God Bless Our Club" Chapter from St. Augustine, Florida participated in an unusual but very successful fund-raiser in Daytona Beach. During "bike week," when thousands of motorcyclists come to town, this Precious Moments Chapter worked with several other organizations to sell raffle tickets for a new motorcycle. It had been generously donated by the Harley-Davidson company. Ticket sales brought in over $100,000, all of which was given to the Easter Seal Society.

Precious Moments Club members are always ready to step in and help whenever they are needed. When Hurricane Andrew devastated southern Florida in 1993, Chapters from all over the country wanted to join the rescue effort. Melinda Liebi, Enesco's consumer relations representative for the Florida region, worked with a local retailer to coordinate collecting funds. The Montessori School in Homestead, Florida, which was virtually destroyed by the storm, was chosen as the recipient of funds sent from Chapters as far away as Montana and Oregon. These generous donations were used to purchase over 200 books to help rebuild the school library.

"We applaud these tangible examples of caring and sharing. They're proof that the true meaning of Precious Moments messages is being heard around the country and around the world."

—Gene Freedman

When the nephew of two members of the "I Believe In Miracles" Chapter in East Walpole, Maine was diagnosed with leukemia, Chapter members raised money for the family. Inspired by their ability to help, this Chapter now makes annual contributions to families with ill or disabled children.

In Washington, "Yakima Valley's Growing Love," "Friends-A-Gathering," and other Chapters organize picnics to help raise money. A four-dollar ticket buys lunch, a goody bag, and a chance to participate in raffles and events such as the ever-popular gum-blowing contest.

Precious Moments collectors and Chapter members always look after each other. When a member of the "Good Friends Are Forever" Chapter in Carrollton, Texas was hospitalized and needed blood transfusions, the other members responded by donating blood for her.

When they realized that if one member had this need, others might be in the same predicament, they set up the Precious Moments Blood Bank to be available to any Precious Moments Club member who needed it.

The members were so enthused over this project that they enlisted the help of two other Chapters in the area, "Let Love Reign," from Hurst and "Birds Of A Feather" from Mesquite. Together the Chapters set up blood banks at three different Texas hospitals.

The "Let Love Reign" Chapter also supports the All Church Home for Children. Every Easter the Chapter donates enough money for each child to have a new Easter outfit. And in the fall, each child is taken to a nearby store and allowed to choose one new pair of shoes to wear to school. In an effort to help the children fit in with their peers as well as possible, no price limit is put on the shoes; the kids can select any pair they want.

Club members contribute not only their money but their time as well. Three Chapters in Tennessee, "The East Tennessee Precious Moments Club," "Friendship Hits The Spot," and "Sharing The Good News In Memphis," combined forces to spend a day with campers at the Tennessee Easter Seal campgrounds in Mt. Joliet. Members and campers enjoyed games, contests, arts and crafts, and everyone left richer for the experience.

"Butcher's Late Bloomers" Chapter from Grand Rapids, Michigan arranged for the costumed character, Uncle Sam to visit the Ken-O-Sha School for disabled children. Each child had his or her Polaroid photograph taken with the jolly, larger-than-life-size character.

The Precious Moments Chapters in the Dallas–Ft. Worth area often work together. One of their favorite projects is the Belmont Assisted Living Retirement Home for older citizens who do not require nursing care. Every Saturday Chapter members go to the home and run a bingo game. Prizes, ranging from a soft drink to a bar of soap, are awarded. Residents say it is the highlight of their week.

The Precious Moments costumed characters often help out with charitable functions and community service activities.

The Precious Moments Family

Collectors have not only become sources of love and strength for one another, they have also adopted Gene Freedman, Sam Butcher, and the entire Enesco staff as their good friends.

Good communication is a high priority for the Enesco Precious Moments family. To keep in better touch with the collectors, Enesco has consumer relations representatives in every region of the country. Under the leadership of Executive Director Bob Feller, they tackle a variety of jobs with unwavering grace and goodwill. They help with planning events and fund-raising projects, and often become friend, den-mother, and confidante to the collectors they meet.

Public appearances are a big part of their job; they are frequent speakers at various community functions, including Parent-Teacher Association meetings, banquets, church groups, and senior citizens organizations. They also often appear on local and national television and radio programs.

When Enesco representatives are asked what their favorite aspect of the job is, their answer is unanimous: "The collectors!"

"Precious Moments collectors are the nicest people in the world, and working with them is the most rewarding part of my job," consumer representative Cheryl Batzing says. "These people have a real feeling for the collection and for other collectors."

Enesco's consumer relations team.

Top Row: Ann Gembala, Mary Rogers, Colleen Kehres, Angie Peterson, Sarah Doran, Bob Feller, Paula Hayden, Laurie Pietrzak.

Middle Row: Stacey Haslett, Sandra Huskey, Angela Thomas, Cheryl Batzing, Melinda Liebi.

Bottom Row: Anita McAvoy, Joni Mack, Lara Brown, Amy Farnan.

"The chapel is my gift of thanksgiving to the Lord for all that He has given me. It is also my gift to everyone who appreciates Precious Moments, so that they might come and see the expressions of my love for the Lord."

—Sam Butcher

The Precious Moments Chapel

In 1984 Sam decided it was time to leave Grand Rapids, Michigan. Sam wanted to settle somewhere where he could completely devote himself to his family and to his art. In February that year, on the way home from a gift show in California, he began searching for the right place.

While staying at a Ramada Inn near Joplin, Missouri, Sam awoke with a feeling that he was somewhere special. Later that day, a real estate agent showed him a house overlooking Center Creek near Carthage, Missouri, and Sam knew he had found his home.

For many years Sam had harbored a dream of building a chapel where he could share his faith and spread the word of God. The idea originated on a visit to the Sistine Chapel in Rome; he was overwhelmed with inspiration by the sight of Michelangelo's masterpiece. He can remember thinking, "Could it be that someday God might grant me the privilege of sharing what light He has given me by painting what I feel He has to say about His grace?"

Sam's wish came true when he moved to Carthage. There, he was finally able to begin construction on the chapel of his dreams.

Hallelujah Square, *which illustrates a child's vision of heaven, is one of the most colorful and evocative of all the murals. Sam has been known to add a child to the mural when he is particularly touched by someone's story.*

The painted murals are one of the most beautiful elements of the chapel. These large paintings cover a total of almost 5,000 square feet. The largest mural is on the ceiling, which spans 2,600 square feet. Sam had to lie on his back on a scaffold nearly thirty-five feet in the air, working for hundreds of hours, to complete the painting.

All the murals and stained glass on the chapel's eastern side depict the Bible's Old Testament stories; New Testament stories are shown on the western side.

Sam and a young visitor share a joyful moment on the Avenue of the Angels.

The walkway lined with Precious Moments angels is called "Avenue of the Angels." Parents often photograph their own little angels beside these Precious Moments statues.

The gallery at the chapel houses displays that change frequently. Some of the most popular exhibits are the "History of Precious Moments," which includes the Esther Everly room, where every porcelain bisque figurine in the collection is shown; a private collection of Sam's art and memorabilia; and an exhibit of handmade gifts and crafts sent to Sam by collectors from across the country.

The gates to the chapel are exquisitely fashioned in wrought iron. Inspiration for the gate design came to Sam as he was relaxing in a coffee shop one evening in Manila. He wanted to start sketching immediately, but had no paper with him, so he began the detailed drawings for the gate on paper napkins.

Unfortunately, over the years, all but one of the napkins was destroyed, burned by flames from the welder's torch. The sole remaining napkin is on display at the chapel. Although the original drawings included angels on the gate, Sam later deleted these, settling on a purely ornamental design.

Sam did the original drawings for the Chapel's majestic wrought iron gates on paper napkins at a coffee shop in Manila.

One of Sam's favorite memories of building the chapel was when the stained glass windows were installed. "The chapel seemed suddenly full of jewels," Sam recalled. Each of the fifteen stained glass windows was carefully created; some contain over 1,200 individually cut pieces of glass. Additional, smaller stained glass windows have been added throughout the chapel. Three of the windows depicting the Beatitudes are shown below.

"Blessed are the meek, for they shall inherit the earth."

"Blessed are the merciful, for they shall obtain mercy."

"Blessed are the pure in heart, for they shall see God."

Sam's patriotism is shared by his children. Philip proudly served his country in the Army.

One of the most moving experiences people have while touring the chapel is visiting the Philip D. Butcher Memorial Room, which Sam designed in honor of the son he lost in an automobile crash on September 6, 1990.

Sam spoke of this room, saying, "Many tears have been shed in Philip's room at the chapel, including mine. After the funeral service for Philip, I had a terrible need inside me, and the way I let it out was to create Philip's room as a tribute to my son, and a place of solace and hope for other people going through troubles and dealing with loss.

"One day I received a letter from a couple who had visited the chapel and stood in Philip's room wondering how I could possibly imagine dealing with the pain, being able to turn it into a creative force. They were so moved. When they arrived home they discovered that while they'd been driving back, their own son had been killed in a car accident. They felt like the hand of God had guided them to the chapel. I was so moved that my pain and loss could help someone else through their own."

The beautiful mural Sam painted in Philip's room shows the young man looking down on his family and friends from a perch in heaven. The hundreds of thousands of visitors who see Philip's room are reminded of Sam's love for his family and of the special bonds that transcend death.

Philip and his wife Connie with (from left) Trisha, Sammy, and Philip, Jr.

He Is My
Inspiration

He Is My Inspiration was created by Sam Butcher as a special chapel figurine. It represents Sam himself, and is wonderfully realistic, as Sam can often be seen with palette in hand, working hard to capture a new Precious Moments character.

Hundreds of thousands of visitors come to the chapel every year. They come to see Sam Butcher's incomparable paintings, they come for inspiration, and they come hoping to meet Sam himself.

One day Sam, covered with paint after working in his studio, wandered out into the chapel garden. A woman stopped him to ask if he was a painter, and he said yes.

They sat and talked for a while and he asked how she liked the chapel, and she answered that she liked it very much. Sam then invited her to join him for lunch at the chapel restaurant. She agreed and they had a pleasant lunch together. As she was getting ready to leave, the woman thanked him, but then added, "You know who I'd really like to have lunch with?"

"Who?" asked Sam.

"Sam Butcher, the artist who created all this beauty."

Sam smiled, stuck out his hand, and said, "You just did!"

Sam says he will always continue to work on the chapel. He tells visitors, "I'm not an artist who feels that he has arrived. I will always find mistakes and feel a need to make corrections."

The chapel is the perfect place for Sam to keep expressing his faith through his abundant creativity. "Many people have asked when the Precious Moments chapel will be finished," says Sam. "I can only say perhaps never . . ."

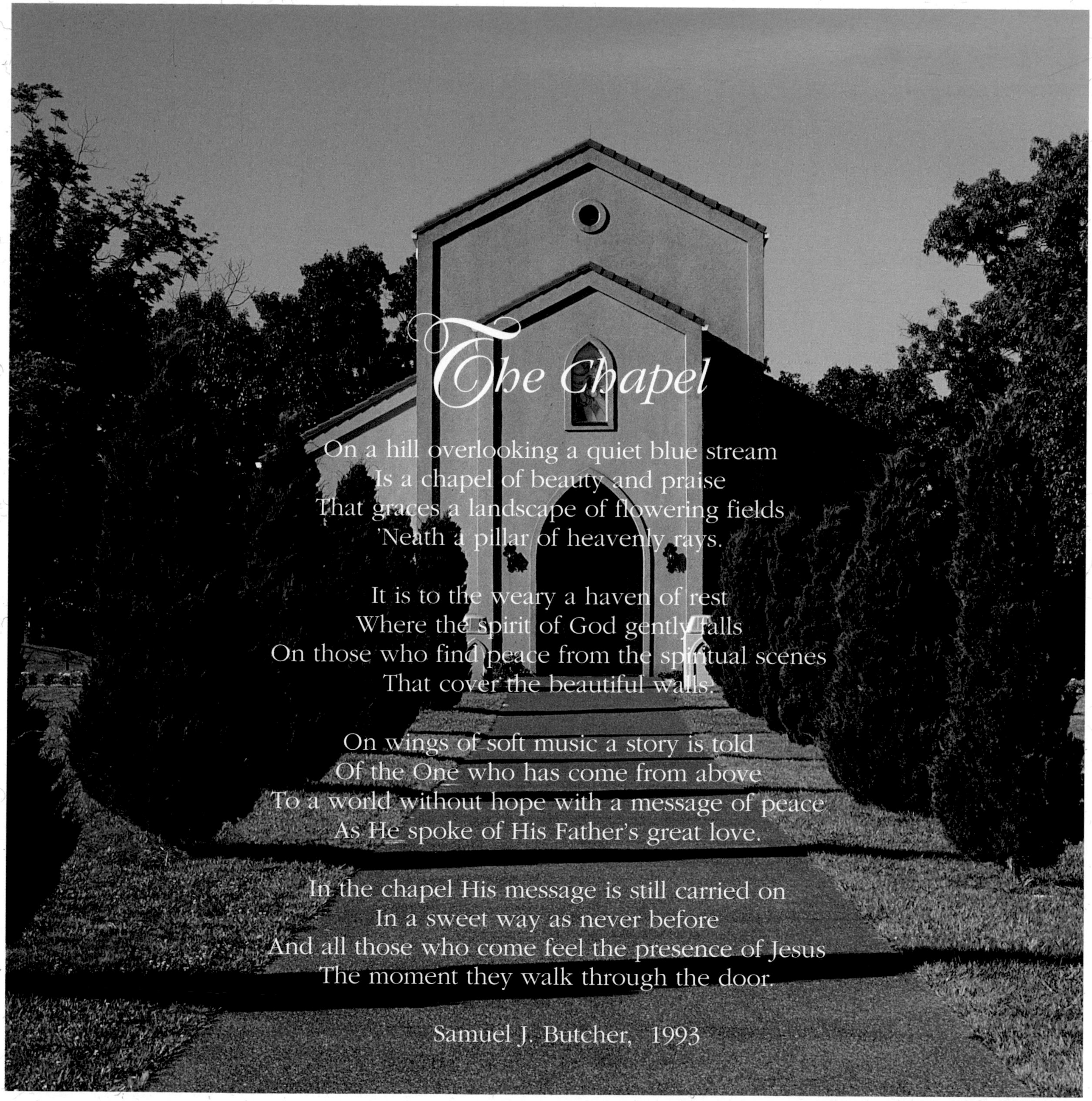

The Chapel

On a hill overlooking a quiet blue stream
Is a chapel of beauty and praise
That graces a landscape of flowering fields
'Neath a pillar of heavenly rays.

It is to the weary a haven of rest
Where the spirit of God gently falls
On those who find peace from the spiritual scenes
That cover the beautiful walls.

On wings of soft music a story is told
Of the One who has come from above
To a world without hope with a message of peace
As He spoke of His Father's great love.

In the chapel His message is still carried on
In a sweet way as never before
And all those who come feel the presence of Jesus
The moment they walk through the door.

Samuel J. Butcher, 1993

The Enesco Precious Moments Collection

A complete pictorial review of America's most endearing and enduring collectible.

This figurine, created in 1993 to commemorate the fifteenth anniversary of the Collection, was named Figurine of the Year by the National Association of Limited Edition Dealers.

15 Years Tweet Music Together
#530840

15 Happy Years Together What A Tweet
#530786

The Enesco
Precious Moments Collection
#230448

Collection Plaque
#E6901

Contents

A
B
C
G
F
Just for you

A friend is someone who cares, who is always there when you need them, who becomes a life-long treasure. Precious Moments gifts of friendship express the affection, loyalty, and devotion between good friends; they warm the heart and touch the soul with their inspiring messages.

A. **To Thee With Love**
#E3120 Suspended

B. **I'm So Glad That God Has Blessed Me With A Friend Like You**
#523623

C. **There Is No Greater Treasure Than To Have A Friend Like You**
#521000

D. **So Glad I Picked You As A Friend**
#524379
1994 Spring Catalog Exclusive Figurine

E. **To My Deer Friend**
#100048

F. **You Are Such A Purr-fect Friend**
#524395

G. **Happiness Is At Our Fingertips**
#529931
1993 Spring Catalog Exclusive Figurine

H. **Friends To The Very End**
#526150 New Introduction

A. To My Forever Friend
#100072

B. Good Friends Are Forever
#521817

C. Friendship Hits The Spot
#520748

D. Our Friendship Is Soda-licious
#524336

A. **We Need A Good Friend Through The Ruff Times**
#520810 Suspended

B. **That's What Friends Are For**
#521183

C. **Wishing You Were Here**
#526916
Tune: "When You Wish Upon A Star"

D. **May Only Good Things Come Your Way**
#524425

E. **There Shall Be Showers Of Blessings**
#522090

A. My Days Are Blue Without You
#520802 Suspended

B. I Will Always Be Thinking Of You
#523631 New Introduction

C. I Get A Kick Out Of You
#E2827 Suspended

D. Thinking Of You Is What I Really Like To Do
#522287

E. Just A Line To Wish You A Happy Day
#520721

A. **Love Cannot Break A True Friendship**
#E4722 Suspended

B. **Something's Missing When You're Not Around**
#105643 Suspended

C. **Friends Never Drift Apart**
#100250

D. **To Tell The Tooth, You're Special**
#105813 Suspended

A
B
DEAREST
E
H
F
G

C

D

I

Love

Love has many faces, each as unique as those who share its warmth and wonder. Each Precious Moments figurine portrays love with tenderness, sincerity, and inspiration; each message expresses your heartfelt sentiment in a very special way. Through these teardrop-eyed children, love's most precious moments are remembered forever.

A. **Sew In Love**
#106844

B. **Sending You Oceans Of Love**
#532010 New Introduction

C. **Love One Another**
#E1376

D. **Sending My Love Your Way**
#528609 New Introduction
1995 Spring Catalog Exclusive Figurine

E. **My Love Will Never Let You Go**
#103497

F. **Thou Art Mine**
#E3113

G. **I'll Never Stop Loving You**
#521418

H. **Hug One Another**
#521299

I. **Thumb-body Loves You**
#521698

A. It's No Yolk When I Say I Love You
#522104 Suspended

B. You Suit Me To A Tee
#526193 New Introduction

C. You Are The Type I Love
#523542

D. Love Is Kind
#E1379A Suspended

E. You Are My Happiness
#526185
1992 Limited Edition

F. My Warmest Thoughts Are You
#524085

A. My Heart Is Exposed With Love
#520624

B. I Can't Bear To Let You Go
#532037 New Introduction

C. Your Love Is So Uplifting
#520675

D. Love Is From Above
#521841

E. Love Covers All
#12009 Suspended

F. Love Covers All
#12254 Suspended

A. **Love Lifted Me**
#E5201 Suspended

B. **Love Beareth All Things**
#E7158

C. **How Can Two Walk Together Except They Agree**
#E9263 Suspended

D. **Love Is The Glue That Mends**
#104027 Suspended

E. **Love Rescued Me**
#102393

A. **He's The Healer Of Broken Hearts**
#100080

B. **This Too Shall Pass**
#114014

C. **Let Not The Sun Go Down Upon Your Wrath**
#E5203 Suspended

D. **Forgiving Is Forgetting**
#E9252 Suspended

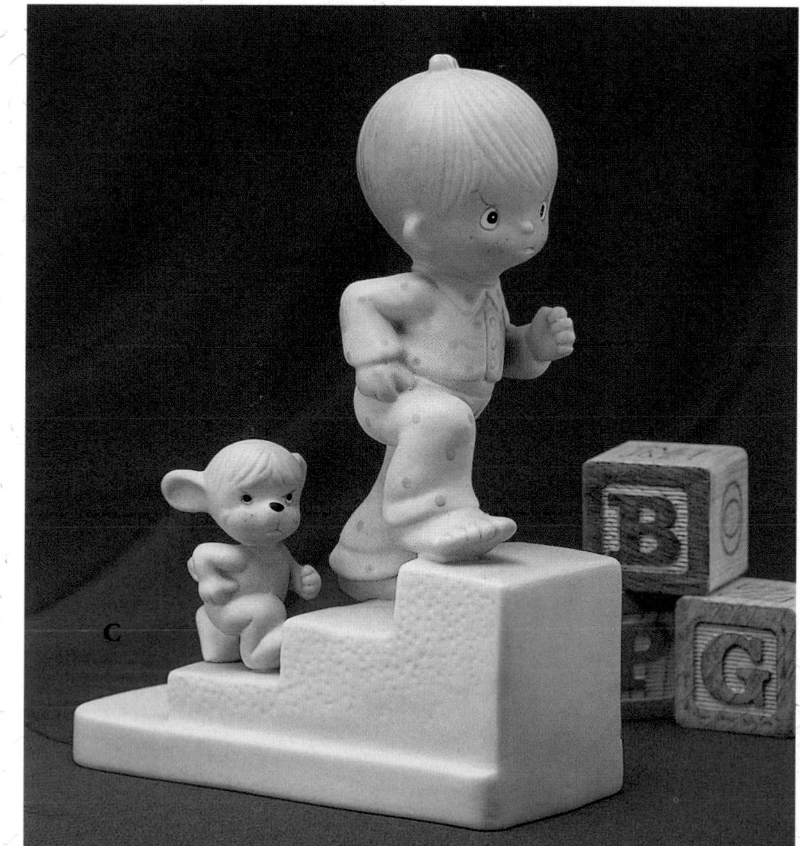

A. **You Are My Number One**
#520829

B. **Sharing Sweet Moments Together**
#526487 New Introduction

C. **Loving Is Sharing**
#E3110G

D. **Puppy Love**
#520764

E. **Sending You My Love**
#109967

F. **Sending My Love**
#100056 Suspended

F

A. **God Is Love, Dear Valentine**
#523518

B. **God Is Love, Dear Valentine**
#E7154 Suspended

C. **Loving You**
#12025 Suspended

D. **Loving You**
#12017 Suspended

E. **God Is Love, Dear Valentine**
#E7153 Suspended

F. **God Is Love, Dear Valentine**
#100625 Suspended

D

B

E

C

F

A

Wedding and Anniversary

On the day you exchanged vows, you shared the promise of forever, and with each passing year, that promise is recalled and renewed. Whether for yourself, or for a couple you hold dear, this time-honored commitment is eloquently expressed through these beautiful figurines, which rekindle each wonderful moment of a life together.

A. **Junior Bridesmaid**
#E2845
5th Issue In The Bridal Party Series

B. **Bridesmaid**
#E2831
1st Issue In The Bridal Party Series

C. **Flower Girl**
#E2835
3rd Issue In The Bridal Party Series

D. **Wedding Arch**
#102369 Suspended

E. **Bride**
#E2846
7th Issue In The Bridal Party Series

F. **Groom**
#E2837
6th Issue In The Bridal Party Series

G. **Best Man**
#E2836
2nd Issue In The Bridal Party Series

H. **Ring Bearer**
#E2833
4th Issue In The Bridal Party Series

G

H

A. **This Is The Day Which The Lord Hath Made**
#E2838
1987 Limited Edition

B. **The Lord Bless You And Keep You**
#E3114

C. **The Lord Bless You And Keep You**
#532118 New Introduction

D. **God Bless Our Family**
#100498
Parents of the Groom

E. **God Bless Our Family**
#100501
Parents of the Bride

A. **The Lord Bless You And Keep You**
#100633 Suspended

B. **The Lord Bless You and Keep You**
#E7179 Suspended

C. **The Lord Bless You And Keep You**
#E7166 Suspended

D. **The Lord Bless You And Keep You**
#E7167 Suspended

E. **The Lord Bless You And Keep You**
#E7180
Tune: "Wedding March By Mendelssohn"

F. **The Lord Bless You And Keep You**
#E5216 Suspended

A. God Bless The Bride
#E2832

B. Sharing Our Joy Together
#E2834 Suspended

C. The Lord Is Your Light
To Happiness
#520837

D. Bless You Two
#E9255

E. Sealed With A Kiss
#524441

A. **Wishing You A Perfect Choice**
#520845

B. **With This Ring I...**
#104019

C. **Precious Memories**
#E2828

D. **Heaven Bless Your Togetherness**
#106755

E. **Wishing You Roads Of Happiness**
#520780

A. **Puppy Love Is From Above**
#106798

B. **God Blessed Our Year Together With So Much Love And Happiness**
#E2854

C. **God Blessed Our Years Together With So Much Love And Happiness**
#E2853

D. **I Still Do**
#531006 New Introduction

E. **I Still Do**
#530999 New Introduction

F. **Precious Memories**
#106763

A. God Blessed Our Years Together With So Much Love And Happiness
#E2855

B. God Blessed Our Years Together With So Much Love And Happiness
#E2856

C. God Blessed Our Years Together With So Much Love And Happiness
#E2857

D. God Blessed Our Years Together With So Much Love And Happiness
#E2859

E. God Blessed Our Years Together With So Much Love And Happiness
#E2860

A
B
D
E
F
Holy
Bible
Potter

Baby and New Mother

The joy of a new baby is unequalled. This tiny gift from God brings hope for the future and a promise fulfilled. With abundant love and caring, you want to give this new life every opportunity, every advantage. Representing your loving devotion, these Precious Moments figurines will be treasured by the family now and for years to come.

C

G

H.

A. **Rejoicing With You**
#E7172 Suspended

B. **Rejoicing With You**
#E4724

C. **Heaven Bless You**
#100285 Suspended
Tune: "Brahms' Lullaby"

D. **Joy On Arrival**
#523178

E. **The Good Lord Always Delivers**
#523453

F. **Blessed Are The Pure In Heart**
#E3104 Suspended

G. **A Special Delivery**
#521493

H. **Heaven Bless You**
#520934

A. **But Love Goes On Forever**
#E3115

B. **My Guardian Angel**
#E5207 Suspended

C. **The Hand That Rocks The Future**
#E5204
"Tune: "Mozart's Lullaby"

D. **The Hand That Rocks The Future**
#E3108 Suspended
Tune: "Brahms' Lullaby"

E. **My Guardian Angel**
#E5205 Suspended
Tune: "Brahms' Lullaby"

F. **My Guardian Angel**
#E5206 Suspended
Tune: "Brahms' Lullaby"

A. **My Guardian Angel**
#E7169 Suspended

B. **My Guardian Angel**
#E7168 Suspended

C. **Safe In The Arms Of Jesus**
#521922
Child Evangelism Fellowship Figurine

D. **God's Precious Gift**
#12041 Suspended

E. **God's Precious Gift**
#12033 Suspended

A. **Jesus Loves Me**
#E1372G

B. **Jesus Loves Me**
#E9279

C. **Jesus Loves Me**
#E9278

D. **Jesus Loves Me**
#E5209 Suspended

E. **Jesus Loves Me**
#E7171 Suspended

F. **Jesus Loves Me**
#E9281 Suspended

A. **Jesus Loves Me**
#E5208 Suspended

B. **Jesus Loves Me**
#E7170 Suspended

C. **Jesus Loves Me**
#E9280 Suspended

D. **Jesus Loves Me**
#E9275 Suspended

E. **Jesus Loves Me**
#E9276 Suspended

F. **Jesus Loves Me**
#E1372B

A. **Baby Boy Crawling**
#E2852E

B. **I Would Be Sunk Without You**
#102970

C. **Baby Girl Lying Down**
#E2852F

D. **A Tub Full Of Love**
#104817

E. **A Tub Full Of Love**
#112313

A. **Sitting Pretty**
#104825 Suspended

B. **Baby Girl Clapping**
#E2852D

C. **Baby Girl Standing**
#E2852B

D. **Baby Boy Sitting**
#E2852C

E. **Baby Boy Standing**
#E2852A

Baby's First Series

A. **Baby's First Trip**
#16012 Suspended
4th Issue In The Baby's First Series

B. **Baby's First Picture**
#E2841 Retired 1986
2nd Issue In The Baby's First Series

C. **Baby's First Meal**
#524077
6th Issue In The Baby's First Series

D. **Baby's First Step**
#E2840 Suspended
1st Issue In The Baby's First Series

A. **Baby's First Haircut**
#12211 Suspended
3rd Issue In The Baby's First Series

B. **Baby's First Word**
#527238 Suspended
7th Issue In The Baby's First Series

C. **Baby's First Birthday**
#524069 Suspended
8th Issue In The Baby's First Series

D. **Baby's First Pet**
#520705 Suspended
5th Issue In The Baby's First Series

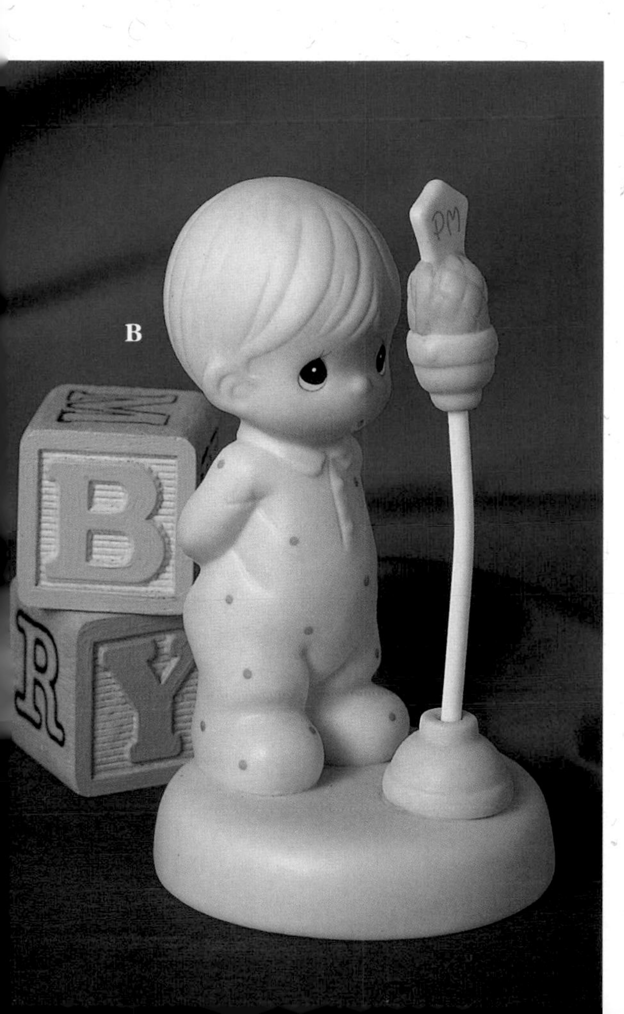

A
B
C
D
TIPPY
Red
OUR HOUSE

Family

Family is the heart of the Precious Moments Collection, just as family is the center of our lives. Expressions of love, understanding, encouragement, and compassion convey the feelings that are sometimes difficult to put into words — even within the family. Dad and Mom. Son and daughter. Sister and brother. Grandma. Grandpa. There's an inspiring Precious Moments collectible that will touch each heart.

A. **The Good Lord Has Blessed Us Tenfold**
#114022
10th Anniversary Commemorative Figurine
1988 Limited Edition

B. **Bless This House**
#E7164 Suspended

C. **To A Very Special Mom**
#E2824

D. **God Bless Our Home**
#12319

E. **God Bless The Day We Found You**
#100153R
(Formerly #100153 Suspended)

F. **God Bless The Day We Found You**
#100145R
(Formerly #100145 Suspended)

G. **To A Special Dad**
#E5212

A. **Part Of Me Wants To Be Good**
#12149 Suspended

B. **To A Very Special Sister**
#528633 New Introduction

C. **To A Very Special Sister**
#E2825

D. **To My Favorite Paw**
#100021 Suspended

E. **Happy Birthday Poppy**
#106836 Suspended

A. **Thinking Of You Is What I Really Like To Do**
#531766 New Introduction
Dated 1994
1st Issue In The Mother's Day Series

B. **The Perfect Grandpa**
#E7160 Suspended

C. **To A Special Mum**
#521965

D. **I Picked A Very Special Mom**
#100536
1987 Limited Edition

E. **Mommy, I Love You**
#112143

F. **Mommy, I Love You**
#109975

A. **The Purr-fect Grandma**
#E7184 Suspended
Tune: "Always In My Heart"

B. **The Purr-fect Grandma**
#E3109

C. **Mother Sew Dear**
#13293

D. **The Purr-fect Grandma**
#13307

E. **The Purr-fect Grandma**
#E7242 Suspended

F. **The Purr-fect Grandma**
#E7183 Suspended

A. **Mother Sew Dear**
#E7182
Tune: "You Light Up My Life"

B. **Mother Sew Dear**
#E3106

C. **Mother Sew Dear**
#E7181 Suspended

D. **Mother Sew Dear**
#E7241 Suspended

E. **Loving Thy Neighbor**
#E2848
Limited Edition of 15,000
4th Issue In The Mother's Love Series

F. **The Purr-fect Grandma**
#E7173
Limited Edition of 15,000
2nd Issue In The Mother's Love Series

G. **The Hand That Rocks The Future**
#E9256
Limited Edition of 15,000
3rd Issue In The Mother's Love Series

H. **Mother Sew Dear**
#E5217
Limited Edition of 15,000
1st Issue In The Mother's Love Series

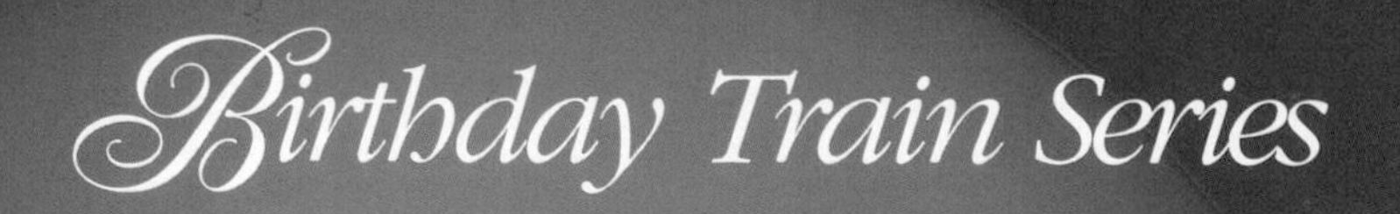

A

B

C

E

F

I

J

K

Birthday

Birthdays are always joyful celebrations at any age—celebrations to share and to remember all year long. Whether you're marking baby's first birthday or Great-grandma's 100th, the most beloved remembrance is always a Precious Moments gift of love . . . right from your heart to theirs.

A. **Bless The Days Of Our Youth**
#16004

B. **May Your Birthday Be Mammoth**
#521825

C. **Being Nine Is Just Divine**
#521833

D. **Isn't Eight Just Great**
#109460

E. **May Your Birthday Be Gigantic**
#15970

F. **This Day Is Something To Roar About**
#15989

G. **Keep Looking Up**
#15997

H. **Wishing You Grr-eatness**
#109479

I. **Heaven Bless Your Special Day**
#15954

J. **God Bless You On Your Birthday**
#15962

K. **Happy Birthday Little Lamb**
#15946

L. **May Your Birthday Be Warm**
#15938

A. Hello World
#521175

B. How Can I Ever Forget You
#526924

C. Friends To The End
#104418 Suspended

D. Brighten Someone's Day
#105953 Suspended

E. Can't Be Without You
#524492

F. Hope You're Over The Hump
#521671

G. Not A Creature Was Stirring
#524484 Suspended
2 PC Set

H. Let's Be Friends
#527270

A. **To My Favorite Fan**
#521043 Suspended

B. **I Only Have Arms For You**
#527769

C. **Happy Birdie**
#527343

D. **Oinky Birthday**
#524506 New Introduction

E. **Wishing You A Happy Bear Hug**
#520659 New Introduction

F. **May Your Birthday Be A Blessing**
#524301

G. **May Your Birthday Be A Blessing**
#E2826 Suspended

H. **This Is The Day Which The Lord Has Made**
#12157 Suspended

I. **May Your Every Wish Come True**
#524298

A
B
E
D
F

Clowns

When Sam Butcher created the teardrop-eyed clowns for the Precious Moments Collection, he knew that nothing renews the spirit and lightens the heart like the joy of laughter. And who better to carry the message of Loving, Caring, and Sharing to those seeking comfort and joy than these messengers of good will. Through them, Sam has found new avenues on which his heart-warming thoughts can travel.

A. **A Friend Is Someone Who Cares**
#520632

B. **Lord, Help Me Make The Grade**
#106216 Suspended

C. **Let's Keep In Touch**
#102520
Tune: "Be A Clown"

D. **Girl Clown**
#12238D

E. **Happy Days Are Here Again**
#104396 Suspended

F. **Girl Clown**
#12238B

G. **Boy Clown**
#12238C

H. **Boy Clown**
#12238A

I. **Clown Thimbles**
#100668 Suspended
2 PC Set

C

I

G

H

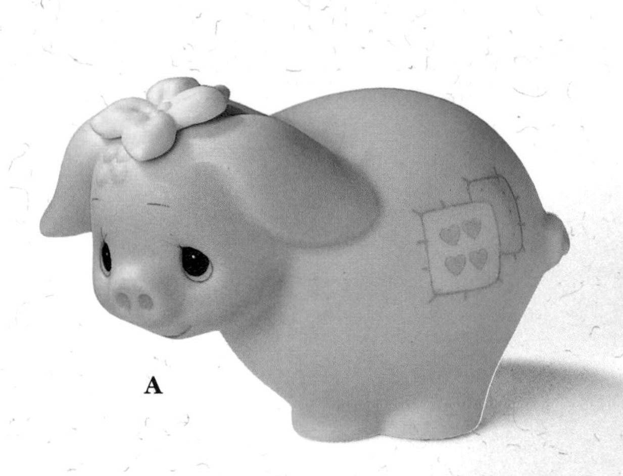

A. **Pig With Patches**
#E9267F Suspended

B. **Lord, Keep Me On The Ball**
#12270
4th Issue In The Clown Series

C. **I Get A Bang Out Of You**
#12262
1st Issue In The Clown Series

D. **The Lord Will Carry You Through**
#12467 Retired 1988
3rd Issue In The Clown Series

E. **Waddle I Do Without You**
#12459 Retired 1989
2nd Issue In The Clown Series

F. **Forever Friends**
#E9283 Suspended
2 PC Set

G. **I'm Falling For Some Bunny And It Happens To Be You/ Our Love Is Heaven-scent**
#E9266 Suspended
2 PC Set

A. **Especially For Ewe**
#E9282C Suspended

B. **You're Worth Your Weight In Gold**
#E9282B Suspended

C. **To Some Bunny Special**
#E9282A Suspended

D. **Dog**
#E9267B Suspended

E. **Bunny**
#E9267C Suspended

F. **Kitten**
#E9267D Suspended

G. **Teddy Bear**
#E9267A Suspended

H. **Lamb**
#E9267E Suspended

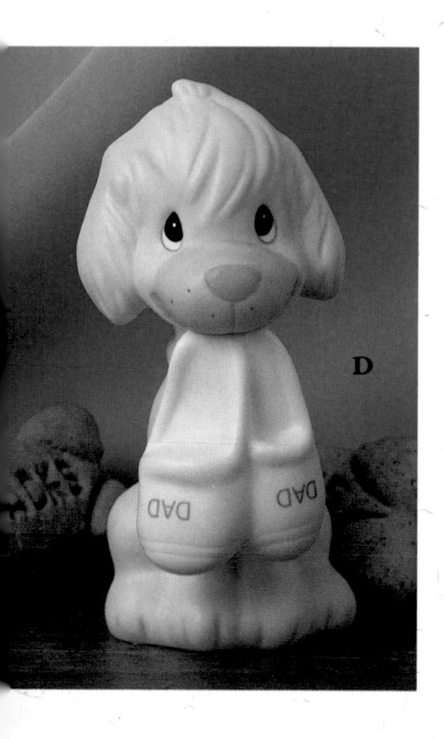

Sammy's
CIRCUS
Welcome
B
A
Sammy's
CIRCUS
E
Sammy's
CIRCUS
F
G
Figurines Sold Separately

Sammy's Circus

The Backyard Big Top

How fondly we recall the childhood make-believe games shared with friends in the backyards that became arenas for our young imaginations. Sam Butcher has watched his thirteen beloved grandchildren at play in games of pretend not unlike his own. Now he pays tribute to children everywhere in the warm and wonderful backyard big top of *Sammy's Circus*. The story is touching, the scene enchanting, the moment inspiring; *Sammy's Circus* will make you remember your own backyard fun.

Sammy's Circus Collector's Set
#604070 New Introduction
7 PC Set
(Displayer not included)

A. **Collin**
#529214 New Introduction

B. **Circus Tent**
#528196 New Introduction ♀

C. **Markie**
#528099 New Introduction

D. **Sammy**
#529222 New Introduction
1994 Limited Edition

E. **Sammy's Circus Displayer**
#PMB015 New Introduction

F. **Tippy**
#529192 New Introduction

G. **Katie**
#529184 New Introduction

H. **Dusty**
#529176 New Introduction

A
B
E
D

Graduation

One of life's most important moments is graduation. Whether from junior high, high school, college, or university, graduation is symbolic of growth; it is the moment of entry into the next stage of life. The blessing of this day is poignantly expressed in these beautiful Precious Moments graduation remembrances—an inspiring way to say, "You make us proud!"

A. **Congratulations, Princess**
#106208

B. **To The Apple Of God's Eye**
#522015

C. **God Understands**
#E1379B Suspended

D. **The Lord Bless You And Keep You**
#532126 New Introduction

E. **God Bless You Graduate**
#106194

F. **The Lord Bless You And Keep You**
#532134 New Introduction

A. It's What's Inside That Counts
#E3119 Suspended

B. Love Is Patient
#E9251 Suspended

C. Love Never Fails
#12300

D. Love Is Sharing
#E7162 Suspended

E. The Lord Bless You And Keep You
#E4721

F. The Lord Bless You And Keep You
#E4720 Suspended

A. **The Lord Bless You And Keep You**
#E7178 Suspended

B. **The Lord Bless You And Keep You**
#E7176 Suspended

C. **The Lord Bless You And Keep You**
#E7175 Suspended

D. **The Lord Bless You And Keep You**
#E7177 Suspended

E. **Seek Ye The Lord**
#E9261 Suspended

F. **Seek Ye The Lord**
#E9262 Suspended

B
C
A
F
G
E

Special Wishes

There are so many times in life that you want to let someone know how special they are, what a wonderful thing they have accomplished, or how deeply they have touched the hearts and lives of others. These are life's precious moments . . . and they usually happen without fanfare or applause. It's then that you know that only a Precious Moments figurine can express the feelings you want to share.

A. **A Poppy For You**
#604208 New Introduction

B. **Dreams Really Do Come True**
#128309 New Introduction

C. **Bon Voyage!**
#522201

D. **Good News Is So Uplifting**
#523615

E. **Sending You A Rainbow**
#E9288 Suspended

F. **Happy Trip**
#521280 Suspended

G. **Cheers To The Leader**
#104035

H. **God Bless You With Rainbows**
#16020 Suspended

I. **You Deserve An Ovation**
#520578

A. **You Have Touched So Many Hearts**
#527661
(Includes Kit For Personalization)

B. **You Have Touched So Many Hearts**
#112577
Tune: "Everybody Loves Somebody"

C. **You Have Touched So Many Hearts**
#E2821

D. **We're In It Together**
#E9259 Suspended

E. **Hallelujah Country**
#105821

F. **Take Heed When You Stand**
#521272 Suspended

A. I Can't Spell Success Without You
#523763 Suspended

B. Thank You For Coming To My Ade
#E5202 Suspended

C. We're Pulling For You
#106151 Suspended

D. High Hopes
#521957 Suspended

E. I Would Be Lost Without You
#526142

F. Angel Of Mercy
#102482

G. It Is Better To Give Than To Receive
#12297 Suspended

A. The End Is In Sight
#E9253 Suspended

B. There's A Light At
The End Of The Tunnel
#521485

C. Time Heals
#523739

D. Hope You're Up
And On The Trail Again
#521205 Suspended

E. Sweep All Your Worries Away
#521779

F. Press On
#E9265

G. Lord, Help Me Stick To My Job
#521450

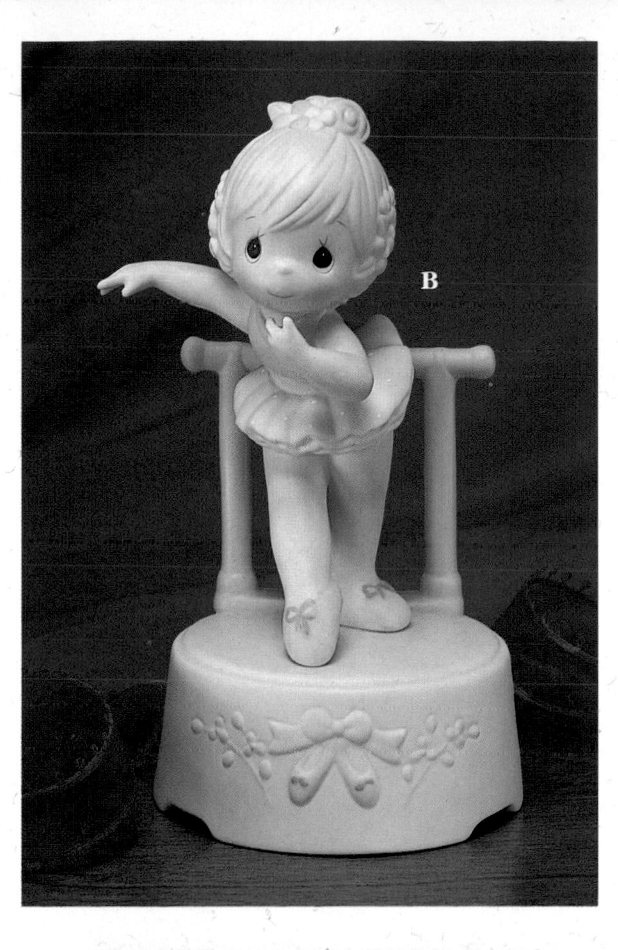

A. **You Can Fly**
#12335 Suspended

B. **Lord, Keep My Life In Balance**
#520691 Suspended
Tune: "Music Box Dancer"

C. **Yield Not To Temptation**
#521310 Suspended

D. **Believe The Impossible**
#109487 Suspended

E. **He Watches Over Us All**
#E3105 Suspended

F. **May Your Life Be Blessed With Touchdowns**
#522023

A

B

C

E

H

God grant me
The serenity
to accept the things
I cannot change,
The courage to change
the things I can, and
The wisdom to know the
difference.

F

G

God grant me
The serenity
to accept the things
I cannot change,
The courage to change
the things I can, and
The wisdom to know the
difference.

I

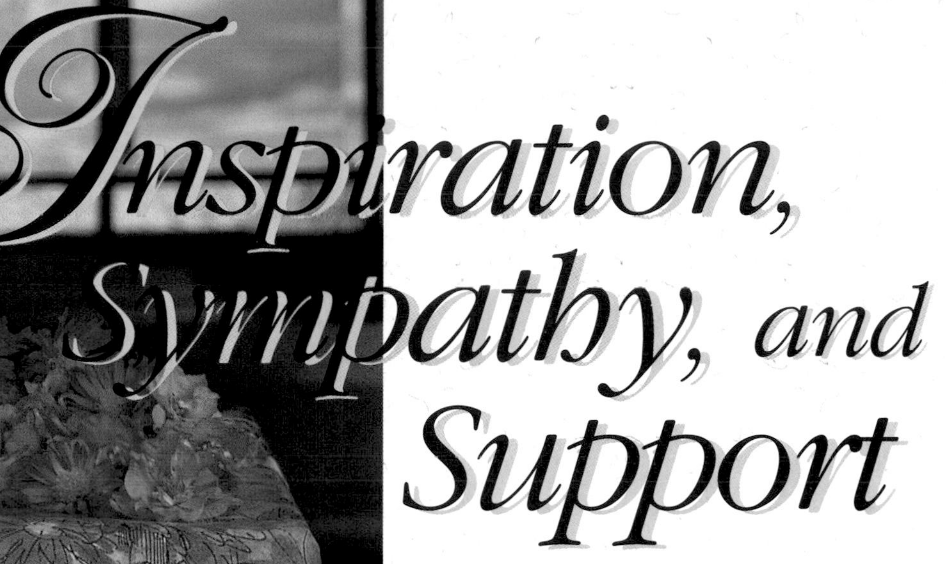

Inspiration, Sympathy, and Support

When you want to say "Take heart and look to Him for guidance," words often seem inadequate. Through these teardrop-eyed figurines, Sam Butcher sends powerful, inspirational messages to be shared with those we love. Each one eloquently expresses the words we cannot find.

A. **The Lord Turned My Life Around**
#520535

B. **Thanking Him For You**
#E7155 Suspended

C. **Vaya Con Dios (Go With God)**
#531146 New Introduction

D. **Prayer Changes Things**
#E5214 Suspended

E. **Prayer Changes Things**
#E5210 Suspended

F. **Prayer Changes Things**
#E1375B Suspended

G. **Get Into The Habit Of Prayer**
#12203 Suspended

H. **Serenity Prayer Girl**
#530697 New Introduction

I. **Serenity Prayer Boy**
#530700 New Introduction

J. **Lord, Give Me Patience**
#E7159 Suspended

K. **Tell It To Jesus**
#521477

L. **The Lord Is Counting On You**
#531707 New Introduction

A. **The Greatest Of These Is Love**
#521868 Suspended

B. **I Believe In The Old Rugged Cross**
#103632

C. **A Reflection Of His Love**
#522279

D. **Onward Christian Soldiers**
#E0523

E. **Make A Joyful Noise**
#E1374G

F. **God Is Love**
#E5213 Suspended

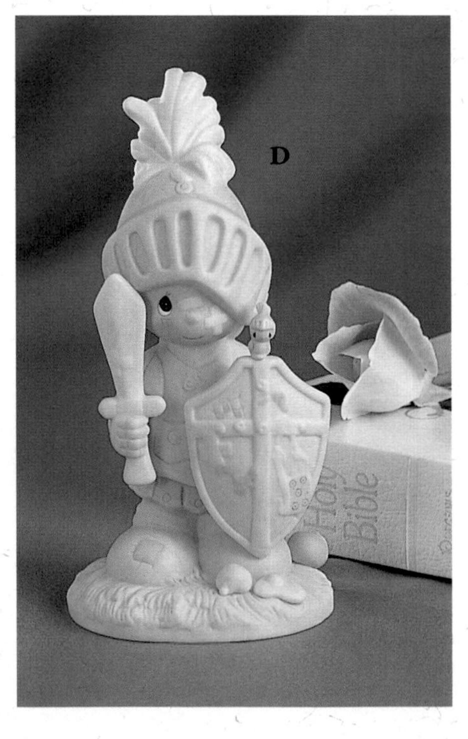

Inspired Thoughts Series

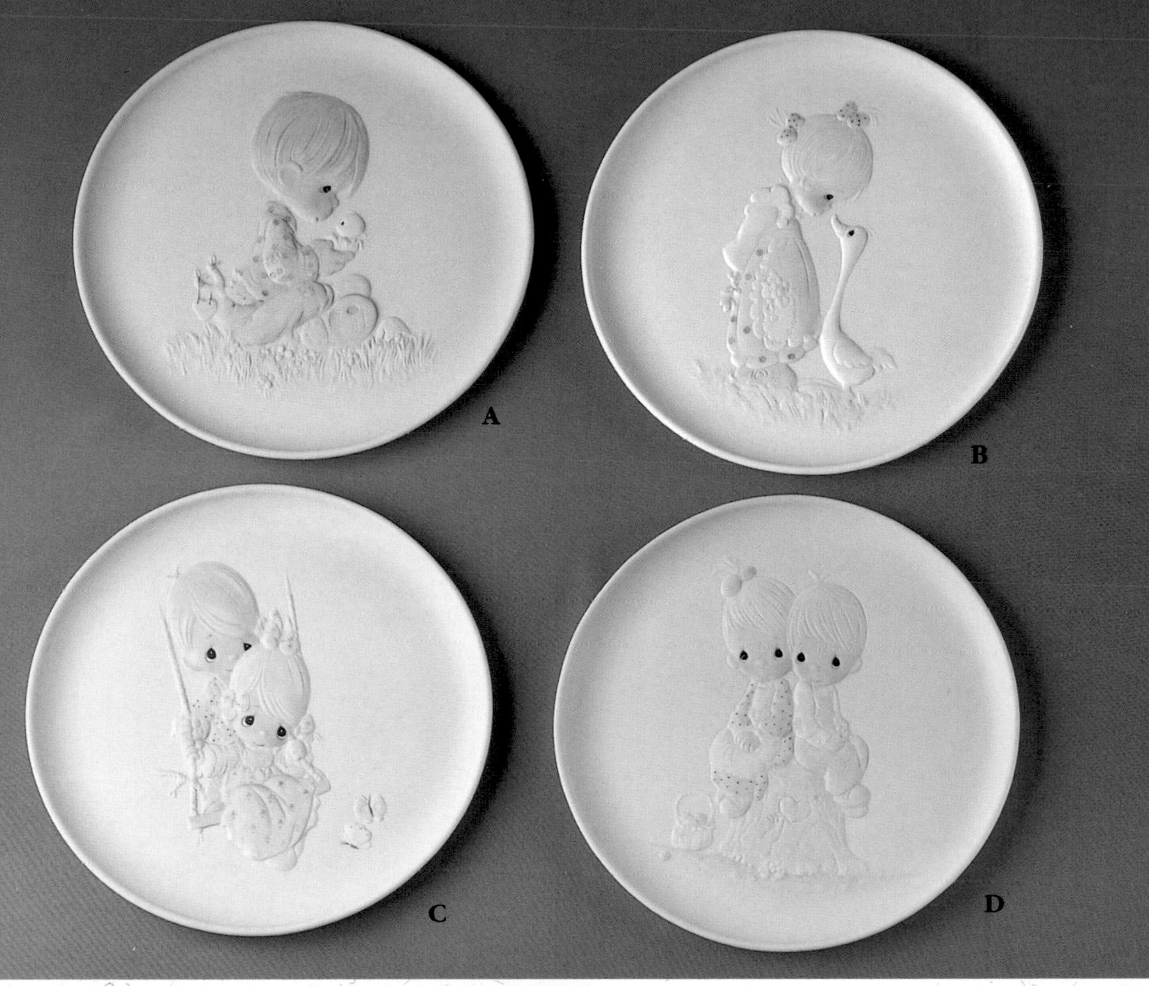

A. **I Believe In Miracles**
#E9257
Limited Edition of 15,000
3rd Issue In The Inspired Thoughts Series

B. **Make A Joyful Noise**
#E7174
Limited Edition of 15,000
2nd Issue In The Inspired Thoughts Series

C. **Love Is Kind**
#E2847
Limited Edition of 15,000
4th Issue In The Inspired Thoughts Series

D. **Love One Another**
#E5215
Limited Edition of 15,000
1st Issue In The Inspired Thoughts Series

E. **We Are All Precious In His Sight**
#102903
1987 Limited Edition

F. **In The Spotlight Of His Grace**
#520543

G. **Lord, Turn My Life Around**
#520551

A. **Lord, Keep My Life In Tune**
#12165 Suspended
Tune: "Amazing Grace"
Rejoice In The Lord Band Series
2 PC Set

B. **Happiness Is The Lord**
#12378 Suspended
Rejoice In The Lord Band Series

C. **Lord, Give Me A Song**
#12386 Suspended
Rejoice In The Lord Band Series

D. **He Is My Song**
#12394 Suspended
Rejoice In The Lord Band Series
2 PC Set

E. **There's A Song In My Heart**
#12173 Suspended
Rejoice In The Lord Band Series

F. **Lord, Keep My Life In Tune**
#12580 Suspended
Tune: "I'd Like To Teach The World To Sing"
Rejoice In The Lord Band Series
2 PC Set

G. **Faith Takes The Plunge**
#111155

H. **He Cleansed My Soul**
#100277

I. **God Is Watching Over You**
#E7163 Suspended

A. **Bear Ye One Another's Burdens**
#E5200 Suspended

B. **No Tears Past The Gate**
#101826

C. **Going Home**
#525979

D. **Lord, I'm Coming Home**
#100110

E. **Bless-um You**
#527335

F. **The Lord Giveth, And The Lord Taketh Away**
#100226

A. **Jesus Is The Only Way**
#520756 Suspended

B. **Bring The Little Ones To Jesus**
#527556
Child Evangelism Fellowship Figurine

C. **Bring The Little Ones To Jesus**
#531359 New Introduction
Child Evangelism Fellowship Plate

D. **To God Be The Glory**
#E2823 Suspended

E. **We Are God's Workmanship**
#E9258

F. **I Belong To The Lord**
#520853 Suspended

A. **The Lord Will Provide**
#523593
1993 Limited Edition

B. **He Upholdeth Those Who Fall**
#E0526 Suspended

C. **Walking By Faith**
#E3117

D. **Trust In The Lord**
#E9289 Suspended

E. **God's Promises Are Sure**
#E9260 Suspended

F. **Hallelujah For The Cross**
#532002 New Introduction

A. **He Loves Me**
#524263
1991 Limited Edition

B. **If God Be For Us, Who Can Be Against Us?**
#E9285 Suspended

C. **The Joy Of The Lord Is My Strength**
#100137

D. **Serving The Lord**
#100161 Suspended

E. **Serving The Lord**
#100293 Suspended

A. **O Worship The Lord**
#102229

B. **O Worship The Lord**
#100064

C. **This Day Has Been Made In Heaven**
#523682
Tune: "Amazing Grace"

D. **May Your Future Be Blessed**
#525316

E. **This Day Has Been Made In Heaven**
#523496

F. **Let The Whole World Know**
#E7165 Suspended

G. **Let The Whole World Know**
#E7186 Suspended
Tune: "What A Friend We Have In Jesus"

A
B
C
F
G
H
HAPPY
EASTER

D E

J

I

The celebration of Easter is commemorated with both deeply inspirational and warm, tender messages . . . each celebrating the Promise fulfilled in a very special way. With messages that touch the heart and soul, each Precious Moments Easter figurine will be a constant reminder of the moment it was received and the blessing it represents, made even more precious because it came from you.

A. **Hoppy Easter, Friend**
#521906

B. **I Will Cherish The Old Rugged Cross**
#523534
Dated 1991

C. **We Are God's Workmanship**
#525960
Dated 1992

D. **Make A Joyful Noise**
#528617
Dated 1993

E. **A Reflection Of His Love**
#529095
Dated 1994

F. **Easter's On Its Way**
#521892

G. **Wishing You A Happy Easter**
#109886

H. **Wishing You A Basket Full Of Blessings**
#109924

I. **Eggspecially For You**
#520667

J. **Love Blooms Eternal**
#127019 New Introduction

THE ENESCO PRECIOUS MOMENTS COLLECTION
Two By Two
The Noah's Ark Story
A
WELCOME
H
Figurines Sold Separately
B
C

Noah's Ark

The parable of Noah and his Ark has inspired old and young through the ages—every glorious rainbow reminds us that the Lord will never again cover the earth in water. Two by two, the animals entered the Ark, and these teardrop-eyed twosomes are a charming re-creation of that long-ago pilgrimage. Noah and his wife accompany them as they set sail toward the rainbow.

D

E

F

G

Noah's Ark Collector's Set
#530948
8 PC Set
(Llamas and displayer not included)

A. **Noah's Ark**
#530042
3 PC Set ♀
(Ark, Noah, wife)

B. **Bunnies**
#530123

C. **Pigs**
#530085

D. **Elephants**
#530131

E. **Sheep**
#530077

F. **Giraffes**
#530115

G. **Llamas**
#531375 New Introduction

H. **Noah's Ark Displayer**
#PMA022

A
B
D
E
NEWS
WAR
CLOSED
STRIKES
RIOTS
UNFAIR
FLOOD

Wishes for the World

Compassion for suffering, prayers for peace, pleas for understanding, patriotic pride. . . these are some of the important messages that Sam Butcher sends the world. Each one is a heartfelt wish, portrayed with simplicity and strength, and every one is an inspiration to live by. As gifts or mementoes, these special figurines are reminders of what the world can be when everyone cares.

A. **What The World Needs Now**
#524352

B. **Jesus Is The Answer**
#E1381R
St. Jude Children's Hospital Figurine
(Formerly E1381 Suspended)

C. **What The World Needs Is Love**
#531065 New Introduction

D. **Lord, Teach Us To Pray**
#524158 New Introduction
1994 Limited Edition
National Day Of Prayer Figurine

E. **Peace Amid The Storm**
#E4723 Suspended

F. **Nothing Can Dampen The Spirit Of Caring**
#603864 New Introduction
1st Issue In The Good Samaritan Series

A. **God Bless The U.S.A.**
#527564
1992 National Day Of Prayer Figurine

B. **God Bless America**
#102938
1986 Limited Edition

C. **America, You're Beautiful**
#528862
1993 National Day Of Prayer Figurine

D. **This Land Is Our Land**
#527777
1992 Limited Edition

E. **Bless Those Who Serve Their Country**
#527521 Suspended
Marine

A. **Bless Those Who Serve Their Country**
#527289 Suspended

B. **Bless Those Who Serve Their Country**
#526568 Suspended
Navy

C. **Bless Those Who Serve Their Country**
#527297 Suspended

D. **Bless Those Who Serve Their Country**
#526576 Suspended
Army

E. **Bless Those Who Serve Their Country**
#526584 Suspended
Air Force

A
B
C
F
Curtains
Blue Lupine
E
SCIENCE
A
PRECIOUS MOMENTS
J
H
I

Calendar Girls

As each month passes, a mood changes, one season ends, and another begins. The calendar is the record by which we measure the passing of the year. Special times, special days, special occasions . . . these are the moments to commemorate and celebrate each month with a Precious Moments Calendar Girl.

A. **January**
#109983

B. **February**
#109991

C. **March**
#110019

D. **April**
#110027

E. **May**
#110035

F. **June**
#110043

G. **July**
#110051

H. **August**
#110078

I. **September**
#110086

J. **October**
#110094

K. **November**
#110108

L. **December**
#110116

A. **Winter's Song**
#12092
1986 Limited Edition
4th Issue In The Four Seasons Figurine Series

B. **Autumn's Praise**
#12084
1986 Limited Edition
3rd Issue In The Four Seasons Figurine Series

C. **Summer's Joy**
#12076
1985 Limited Edition
2nd Issue In The Four Seasons Figurine Series

D. **The Voice Of Spring**
#12068
1985 Limited Edition
1st Issue In The Four Seasons Figurine Series

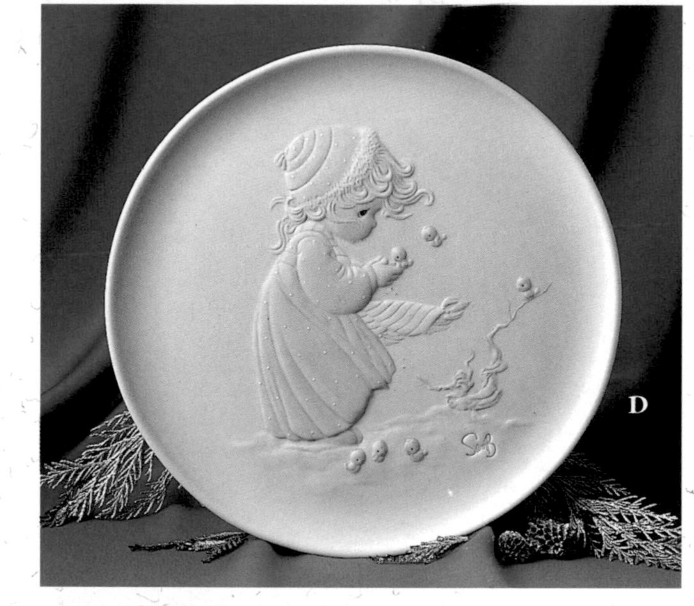

A. **Summer's Joy**
#12114
1985 Limited Edition
2nd Issue In The Four Seasons Plate Series

B. **The Voice Of Spring**
#12106
1985 Limited Edition
1st Issue In The Four Seasons Plate Series

C. **Autumn's Praise**
#12122
1986 Limited Edition
3rd Issue In The Four Seasons Plate Series

D. **Winter's Song**
#12130
1986 Limited Edition
4th Issue In The Four Seasons Plate Series

E. **Four Seasons Thimble Series**
#100641
4 PC Set
1985 Limited Edition

Four Seasons Series
A
B
C
E
F
Summer
Spring

The most beautiful expressions of Loving, Caring, and Sharing are these exquisite collectors' dolls, each one a tender tribute to the joys of childhood and to the different stages of life. Artist Sam Butcher often celebrated the joy of parenthood by creating a doll in honor of a son or daughter. Whatever the occasion, these collectors' dolls will be lasting treasures to be enjoyed for a lifetime.

A. **Winter's Song**
#408778
1990-91 Limited Edition
Tune: "Through The Eyes Of Love"

B. **The Voice Of Spring**
#408786
1990-91 Limited Edition

C. **Summer's Joy**
#408743
1990-91 Limited Edition
Tune: "You Are My Sunshine"

D. **Autumn's Praise**
#408808
1990-91 Limited Edition

E. **Winter's Song**
#408816
1990-91 Limited Edition

F. **The Voice Of Spring**
#408735
1990-91 Limited Edition
Tune: "April Love"

G. **Summer's Joy**
#408794
1990-91 Limited Edition

H. **Autumn's Praise**
#408751
1990-91 Limited Edition
Tune: "Autumn Leaves"

A. **The Eyes Of The Lord Are Upon You**
#429570 Suspended
Tune: "Brahms' Lullaby"

B. **The Eyes Of The Lord Are Upon You**
#429589 Suspended
Tune: "Brahms' Lullaby"

C. **P.D.**
#12475 Suspended

D. **Trish**
#12483 Suspended

E. **Tammy**
#E7267G
Limited Edition of 5,000

F. **Cubby**
#E7267B
Limited Edition of 5,000

A. **Timmy**
#E5397 Suspended

B. **You Have Touched So Many Hearts**
#422282
Tune: "Everybody Loves Somebody"
1991/92 Limited Edition

C. **You Have Touched So Many Hearts**
#427527
1991/92 Limited Edition

D. **Katie Lynne**
#E0539 Suspended

D

A. **Bethany**
#12432 Suspended

B. **Aaron**
#12424 Suspended

C. **May You Have An Old-Fashioned Christmas**
#417777
1991/92 Limited Edition
Tune: "Have Yourself A Merry Little Christmas"

D. **May You Have An Old-Fashioned Christmas**
#417785
1991/92 Limited Edition

E. **Connie**
#102253
Limited Edition of 7,500

A. **Candy**
#100463
Limited Edition of 12,000

B. **Bong Bong**
#100455
Limited Edition of 12,000

C. **Mikey**
#E6214B Suspended

D. **Debbie**
#E6214G Suspended

E. **Kristy**
#E2851 Suspended

F. **Angie, The Angel Of Mercy**
#12491
Limited Edition of 12,500

THE ENESCO
PRECIOUS MOMENTS
COLLECTION
Sugar Town™
D
E
Dr. Sugar
The Doctor is Out
Happy New Year
G
A
B
C
F
K
J
SWEET SHOP
TOYS
IT'S A BOY
Welcome to Sugar Town™
Population 13+1
...and Growing
N

Sugar Town

1994 Introductions

Welcome to *Sugar Town*, one of the sweetest places on Earth. The town is named in honor of the kind family doctor who brought Sam Butcher into the world on New Year's Day 1939—Dr. Sam Sugar. That long-ago morning is endearingly captured in the 1994 Introductions to the series.

Doctor's Office Collector's Set
#529281 New Introduction
1994 Limited Edition
7 PC Set Includes Items C, D, F, G, M, N, P

A. **Lamp Post**
#529559 New Introduction

B. **Mailbox**
#531847 New Introduction

C. **Dr. Sam Sugar**
#529850 New Introduction

D. **Doctor's Office**
#529869 New Introduction

E. **Sam's House**
#530468 New Introduction
1994 Limited Edition

F. **Leon And Evelyn Mae**
#529818 New Introduction

G. **Jan**
#529826 New Introduction

H. **Single Tree**
#533173 New Introduction

I. **Cobblestone Bridge**
#533203 New Introduction

J. **Town Square Clock**
#532908 New Introduction

K. **Straight Sidewalk**
#533157 New Introduction

L. **Double Tree**
#533181 New Introduction

M. **Sugar And Her Doghouse**
#533165 New Introduction
2 PC Set

N. **Stork With Baby Sam**
#529788 New Introduction
1994 Limited Edition

O. **Curved Sidewalk**
#533149 New Introduction

P. **Free Christmas Puppies**
#528064 New Introduction

1993 Introductions

Sam's House Collector's Set
#531774
7 PC Set
(Includes Items A, B, C, D, E, F, G)

A. **Sam's House**
#529605 ♀

B. **Fence**
#529796

C. **Sammy**
#528668

D. **Katy Lynne**
#529524

E. **Sam Butcher**
#529842
1993 Limited Edition

F. **Dusty**
#529435

G. **Sam's Car**
#529443

H. **Sugar Town Chapel**
#530484
1993 Limited Edition

A. Chapel
#529621

B. Christmas Tree
#528684

C. Grandfather
#529516

D. Nativity
#529508

E. Philip
#529494

F. Aunt Ruth & Aunt Dorothy
#529486

G. Sam Butcher
#529567
1992 Limited Edition

Sugar Town Modular Display
#PMB007
To enhance the Sugar Town scenes, you can display the beautiful buildings and figurines on these specially designed bases that join together to form a complete village. Figurines sold separately.

Future Introduction

1994 Introduction

1992 Introduction

1993 Introduction

A
B
D
E
F
G
DO NOT OPEN TILL CHRISTMAS
ORNAMENTS
Egg Nog

Christmas and Thanksgiving

'Tis the season of love, the season of gift-giving, the season of joy and celebration. Christmas is a time for family and friends to gather in front of bright trees and warm fireplaces, in small towns and large cities, to share the year gone by and consider the new year ahead. These are moments to cherish, moments to reflect, and each is very precious.

A. **Oh What Fun It Is To Ride**
#109819

B. **Do Not Open 'Til Christmas**
#522244 Suspended
Tune: "Toyland"

C. **Ring Those Christmas Bells**
#525898

D. **Bringing You A Merry Christmas**
#527599

E. **Merry Christmas Deer**
#522317

F. **Wishing You A Ho, Ho, Ho**
#527629

G. **Dropping In For The Holidays**
#531952 New Introduction

H. **Meowie Christmas**
#109800

I. **Tied Up For The Holidays**
#527580

A. **I'm Sending You A White Christmas**
#E2829

B. **Wishing You A Yummy Christmas**
#109754 Suspended

C. **Just Poppin' In To Say Halo!**
#523755 New Introduction

D. **Now I Lay Me Down To Sleep**
#522058 New Introduction

E. **Halo, And Merry Christmas**
#12351 Suspended

F. **Wishing You A Cozy Season**
#521949 Suspended

G. **Dropping In For Christmas**
#E2350 Suspended

A. **Wishing You A Very Successful Season**
#522120

B. **Wishing You A Merry Christmas**
#E5394 Suspended
Tune: "We Wish You A Merry Christmas"

C. **Christmas Joy From Head To Toe**
#E2361 Suspended

D. **'Tis The Season**
#111163

E. **May Your Christmas Be Delightful**
#15482 Suspended

F. **May Your Christmas Be Cozy**
#E2345 Suspended

G. **May Your Christmas Be Warm**
#E2348 Suspended

E

A. **Our First Christmas Together**
#115290 Suspended

B. **Our First Christmas Together**
#E2377 Suspended

C. **The Fruit Of The Spirit Is Love**
#521213

D. **You Are My Favorite Star**
#527378

E. **Our First Christmas Together**
#E2378 Suspended

F. **But Love Goes On Forever**
#E6118 Suspended
2 PC Set

G. **Sharing Our Christmas Together**
#102490 Suspended

H. **Sharing Our Season Together**
#E0501 Suspended

A. **May You Have The Sweetest Christmas**
#15776 Suspended

B. **Christmas Fireplace**
#524883 Suspended

C. **God Gave His Best**
#15806 Suspended

D. **Silent Night**
#15814 Suspended
Tune: "Silent Night"

E. **Tell Me A Story**
#15792 Suspended

F. **Have A Beary Merry Christmas**
#522856 Suspended

G. **The Story Of God's Love**
#15784 Suspended

A. **Blessings From My House To Yours**
#E0503 Suspended

B. **May Your Christmas Be Blessed**
#E5376 Suspended

C. **The Greatest Gift Is A Friend**
#109231

D. **To A Very Special Mom And Dad**
#521434 Suspended

E. **Good Friends Are For Always**
#524123

F. **It's So Uplifting To Have A Friend Like You**
#524905

G. **Blessed Are The Pure In Heart**
#E0521 Suspended

A. **Tell Me The Story Of Jesus**
#E2349 Suspended

B. **Luke 2:10-11**
#532916 New Introduction

C. **God Cared Enough To Send His Best**
#524476 New Introduction

D. **O Come, All Ye Faithful**
#E2352 Suspended
Tune: "O Come, All Ye Faithful"

E. **Silent Knight**
#E5642 Suspended
Tune: "Silent Night"

F. **Unto Us A Child Is Born**
#E2808 Suspended
Tune: "Jesus Loves Me"

G. **Unto Us A Child Is Born**
#E2013 Suspended

A. **Angels We Have Heard On High**
#524921

B. **He Careth For You**
#E1377B Suspended

C. **He Leadeth Me**
#E1377A Suspended

D. **God Sends The Gift Of His Love**
#E6613 Suspended

E. **Jesus Is The Light That Shines**
#E0502 Suspended

F. **Oh Worship The Lord**
#E5385 Suspended

G. **Oh Worship The Lord**
#E5386 Suspended

A. **The First Noël**
#E2365 Suspended

B. **The First Noël**
#E2366 Suspended

C. **The Light Of The World Is Jesus**
#521507
Tune: "White Christmas"

D. **Ring Out The Good News**
#529966

E. **A Special Chime For Jesus**
#524468

F. **It's The Birthday Of A King**
#102962 Suspended

G. **We Saw A Star**
#12408 Suspended
Tune: "Joy To The World"
3 PC Set

A. **May Your World Be Trimmed With Joy**
#522082

B. **Peace On Earth**
#E2804 Suspended

C. **We're Going To Miss You**
#524913

D. **Perfect Harmony**
#521914 New Introduction

E. **Joy To The World**
#E2344 Suspended
2 PC Set

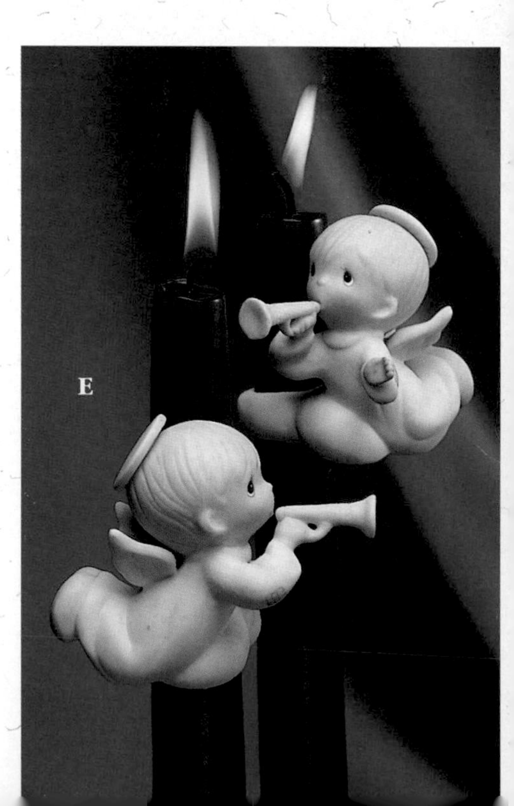

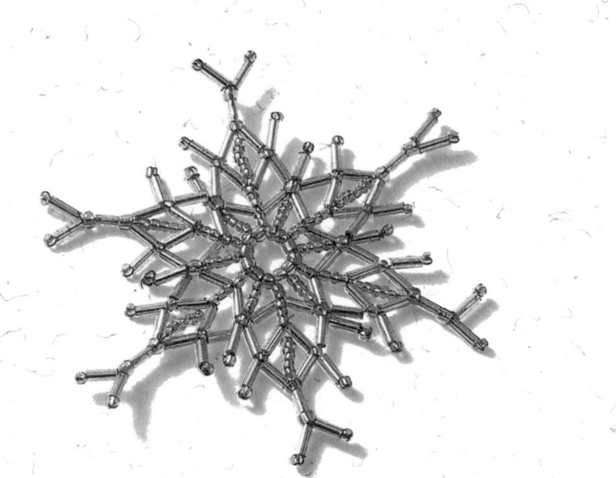

Giving Thanks

E

F

G

A. **Peace On Earth**
#E4726 Suspended
Tune: "Jesus Loves Me"

B. **Peace On Earth**
#E4725 Suspended

C. **Peace On Earth**
#E9287 Suspended

D. **Peace On Earth**
#109746 Suspended
Tune: "Hark, The Herald Angels Sing"

E. **We Gather Together To Ask The Lord's Blessing**
#109762
6 PC Set with cassette

F. **Brotherly Love**
#100544 Suspended

G. **Thank You, Lord, For Everything**
#522031 Suspended

Figurines Sold Separately
A
"Come Let Us Adore Him"
Booklet and Cassette Included with #104000
The Nativity
SILENT NIGHT
AWAY IN A MANGER
WE THREE KINGS
B
E
F
Jesus the Saviour is born
J
K

Nativities

C

D

G

H

I

M

The true meaning of Christmas is inspiringly portrayed in the beautiful Precious Moments Nativity. It's a scene so touching it deserves to be displayed throughout the year. Each teardrop-eyed participant plays a special role in the timeless story that is re-told each year, spreading the joy of the season and the message of peace on Earth and good will to men.

A. **Nativity Displayer**
#PMA077

B. **Nativity Wall**
#E5644
2 PC Set

C. **The Heavenly Light**
#E5637

D. **Rejoice O Earth**
#E5636

E. **We Three Kings**
#E5635
3 PC Set

F. **I'll Play My Drum For Him**
#E2360

G. **Joy To The World**
#E5378 Suspended

H. **Cow**
#E5638

I. **Nativity Cart**
#528072 New Introduction

J. **Have I Got News For You**
#105635 Suspended

K. **Come Let Us Adore Him**
#104000
9 PC Nativity Set with Booklet and Cassette
(Formerly E2800)

L. **Camel**
#E2363

M. **Donkey**
#E5621

A. **Isn't He Wonderful**
#E5640 Suspended

B. **Come Let Us Adore Him**
#E5619 Suspended

C. **Isn't He Wonderful**
#E5639 Suspended

D. **Some Bunny's Sleeping**
#115274

E. **Happy Birthday Dear Jesus**
#524875 Suspended

F. **We Have Come From Afar**
#526959 Suspended

G. **Goat**
#E2364 Suspended

H. **Tubby's First Christmas**
#E0511 Suspended

D

A. **Honk If You Love Jesus**
#15490
2 PC Set

B. **Isn't He Precious**
#E5379

C. **Wishing You A Comfy Christmas**
#527750

D. **Jesus The Savior Is Born**
#520357 Suspended

E. **They Followed The Star**
#E5624
3 PC Set

F. **Jesus Is The Sweetest Name I Know**
#523097 Suspended

G. **It's A Perfect Boy**
#E0512 Suspended

A. **I'll Play My Drum For Him**
#E2355 Suspended
Tune: "The Little Drummer Boy"

B. **I'll Play My Drum For Him**
#E2356 Suspended

C. **They Followed The Star**
#E5641 Suspended

D. **A Monarch Is Born**
#E5380 Suspended

E. **God Sent His Son**
#E0507 Suspended

F. **Let Heaven And Nature Sing**
#E2346 Suspended
Tune: "Joy To The World"

G. **Jesus Is Coming Soon**
#12343 Suspended

H. **His Sheep Am I**
#E7161 Suspended

Actual Size 9" H.

A. **O Come, Let Us Adore Him**
#111333 Suspended
4 PC Set

B. **Come Let Us Adore Him**
#E2810 Suspended
Tune: "Joy To The World"

C. **Wee Three Kings**
#E0520 Suspended
Tune: "We Three Kings Of Orient Are"

D. **Jesus Is Born**
#E2801 Suspended

D

Jesus Is Born

A. **Prepare Ye The Way Of The Lord**
#E0508 Suspended
6 PC Set

B. **We Have Seen His Star**
#E5620 Suspended

C. **Jesus Is Born**
#E5623 Suspended

D. **We Have Seen His Star**
#E2010 Suspended

E. **His Name Is Jesus**
#E5381 Suspended

F. **Crown Him Lord Of All**
#E2807 Suspended
Tune: "O Come, All Ye Faithful"

G. **Crown Him Lord Of All**
#E2803 Suspended

H. **Christmas Is A Time To Share**
#E2802 Suspended

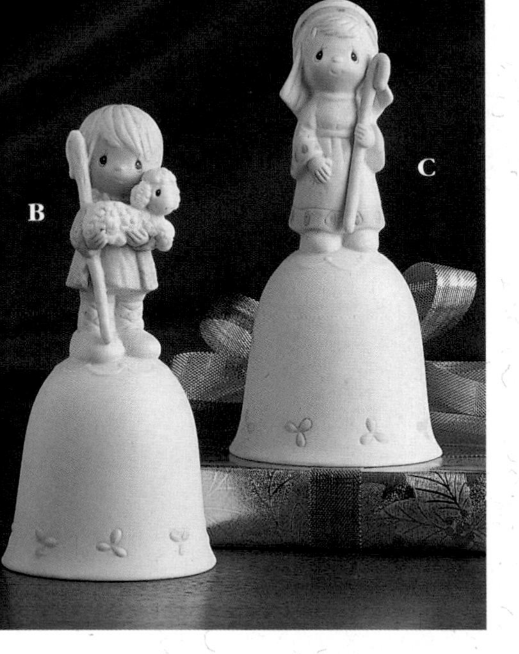

A. **Jesus Is Born**
#E2012 Suspended

B. **Jesus Is Born**
#E2809 Suspended
Tune: "Hark, The Herald Angels Sing"

C. **Bringing God's Blessing To You**
#E0509 Suspended

D. **He Is The Star Of The Morning**
#522252 Suspended

E. **For God So Loved The World**
#E5382 Suspended
4 PC Set

F. **Let Heaven And Nature Sing**
#E2347
2nd Issue In The Christmas Collection Series
Limited Edition of 15,000

G. **Come Let Us Adore Him**
#E5646
1st Issue In The Christmas Collection Series
Limited Edition of 15,000

H. **Wee Three Kings**
#E0538
3rd Issue In The Christmas Collection Series
Limited Edition of 15,000

I. **Unto Us A Child Is Born**
#E5395
4th Issue In The Christmas Collection Series
Limited Edition of 15,000

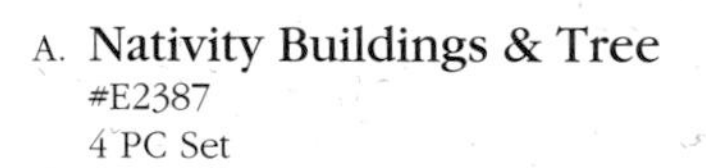

A. **Nativity Buildings & Tree**
#E2387
4 PC Set

B. **Rejoice O Earth**
#520268

C. **Come Let Us Adore Him**
#E2395
11 PC Set

D. **Have I Got News For You**
#528137 New Introduction

D

A

C

A. Mini Nativity Animals
#102296 Suspended
3 PC Set

B. Happy Birthday Jesus
#530492

C. I'll Play My Drum For Him
#E5384

D. It's A Perfect Boy
#525286

E. Isn't He Precious
#522988 Suspended

F. Shepherd Of Love
#102261

G. They Followed The Star
#108243
3 PC Set

H. Some Bunny's Sleeping
#522996 Suspended

I. Tubby's First Christmas
#525278

Ornament Sold Separately

Holiday Ornaments

F

G

K

M

L

There is a tradition in most homes that certain ornaments on the family Christmas tree commemorate special times and special people we hold dear. Each exquisite, inspiring ornament reflects these wonderful times and loving people, and will create treasured memories for Christmases to come.

A. **Bringing You A Merry Christmas**
#528226 New Introduction

B. **Share In The Warmth Of Christmas**
#527211

C. **May Your Christmas Be Delightful**
#15849 Suspended

D. **Have A Heavenly Christmas**
#12416

E. **Sending You A White Christmas**
#528218 New Introduction

F. **May Your Christmas Be Happy**
#15822 Suspended

G. **May All Your Christmases Be White**
#521302 Suspended

H. **Ornament Enhancer**
#603171 New Introduction

I. **Smile Along The Way**
#113964 Suspended

J. **Make A Joyful Noise**
#522910

K. **I'm Sending You A White Christmas**
#112372 Suspended

L. **Dashing Through The Snow**
#521574 Suspended

M. **May God Bless You With A Perfect Holiday Season**
#E5390 Suspended

A. Good Friends Are For Always
#524131

B. You Have Touched So Many Hearts
#112356

C. It's So Uplifting To Have A Friend Like You
#528846

D. To My Forever Friend
#113956

E. Friends Never Drift Apart
#522937

F. Love One Another
#522929

G. My Love Will Never Let You Go
#114006 Suspended

H. Love Rescued Me
#102385

I. Love Is Patient
#E0536 Suspended

J. Love Is Kind
#E5391 Suspended

K. Love Is Patient
#E0535 Suspended

L. Our First Christmas Together
#E2385 Suspended

A. **Mother Sew Dear**
#E0514

B. **The Perfect Grandpa**
#E0517 Suspended

C. **The Purr-fect Grandma**
#E0516

D. **Rocking Horse Hanging Ornament**
#102474 Suspended

E. **Mouse with Cheese Hanging Ornament**
#E2381 Suspended

F. **Baby's First Christmas**
#E2372 Suspended

G. **Baby's First Christmas**
#E5632 Suspended

H. **Baby's First Christmas**
#E5631 Suspended

I. **Baby's First Christmas**
#E2362 Suspended

J. **But Love Goes On Forever**
#E5627 Suspended

K. **But Love Goes On Forever**
#E5628 Suspended

L. **The Good Lord Always Delivers**
#527165 Suspended

M. **To A Special Dad**
#E0515 Suspended

N. **It's A Perfect Boy**
#102415 Suspended

A. **Happiness Is The Lord**
#15830 Suspended

B. **God Sent You Just In Time**
#113972 Suspended

C. **Waddle I Do Without You**
#112364

D. **Honk If You Love Jesus**
#15857 Suspended

E. **Cheers To The Leader**
#113999 Suspended

F. **I'm A Possibility**
#111120 Suspended

G. **Lord, Keep Me On My Toes**
#525332

H. **Trust And Obey**
#102377

I. **Happy Trails Is Trusting Jesus**
#523224 Suspended

J. **Serve With A Smile**
#102458 Suspended

K. **Serve With A Smile**
#102431 Suspended

L. **Angel of Mercy**
#102407

M. **I Believe In The Old Rugged Cross**
#522953 Suspended

N. **He Cleansed My Soul**
#112380

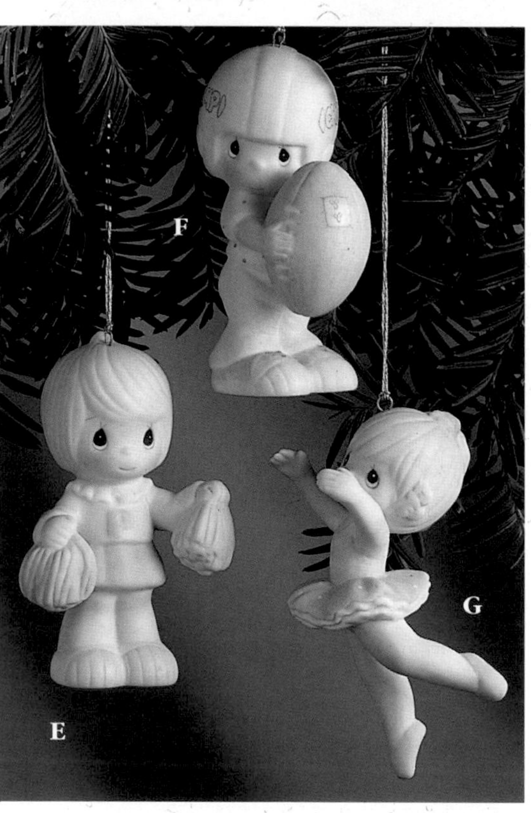

F

A. **Come Let Us Adore Him**
#E5633 Suspended
4 PC Set

B. **Wee Three Kings**
#E5634 Suspcnded
3 PC Set

C. **Manger Animals Hanging Ornaments**
#E2386 Suspended
3 PC Set

D. **Unto Us A Child Is Born**
#E5630 Suspended

E. **Shepherd Of Love**
#102288 Suspended

F. **Onward Christmas Soldiers**
#527327 New Introduction

G. **Jesus Is The Light That Shines**
#E0537 Suspended

H. **The First Noël**
#E2367 Suspended

I. **Tell Me The Story Of Jesus**
#E0533 Suspended

J. **Joy To The World**
#E2343 Suspended

K. **O Come All Ye Faithful**
#E0531 Suspended

L. **Peace On Earth**
#E5389 Suspended

1994
A
Christmas is a time for Love
1994
B
1994
Our first Christmas Together
1994
D
E
1994
F
1994
You are always in my Heart
1994
G
Birthday Series

A. **I'm Nuts About You**
#520411
Dated 1992

B. **Baby's First Christmas**
#527475
Dated 1992

C. **Baby's First Christmas**
#527483
Dated 1992

D. **Our First Christmas Together**
#528870
Dated 1992

E. **But The Greatest Of These Is Love**
#527718
Dated 1992

F. **But The Greatest Of These Is Love**
#527726
Dated 1992

G. **But The Greatest Of These Is Love**
#527734
Dated 1992
4th Issue In The Masterpiece Ornament Series

H. **But The Greatest Of These Is Love**
#527696
Dated 1992

I. **But The Greatest Of These Is Love**
#527688
Dated 1992

A. **Our First Christmas Together**
#522945
Dated 1991

B. **May Your Christmas Be Merry**
#524182
Dated 1991

C. **May Your Christmas Be Merry**
#526940
Dated 1991
3rd Issue In The Masterpiece Ornament Series

D. **May Your Christmas Be Merry**
#524174
Dated 1991

E. **May Your Christmas Be Merry**
#524190
Dated 1991

F. **May Your Christmas Be Merry**
#524166
Dated 1991

G. **Sno-bunny Falls For You Like I Do**
#520438
Dated 1991

H. **Baby's First Christmas**
#527084
Dated 1991

I. **Baby's First Christmas**
#527092
Dated 1991

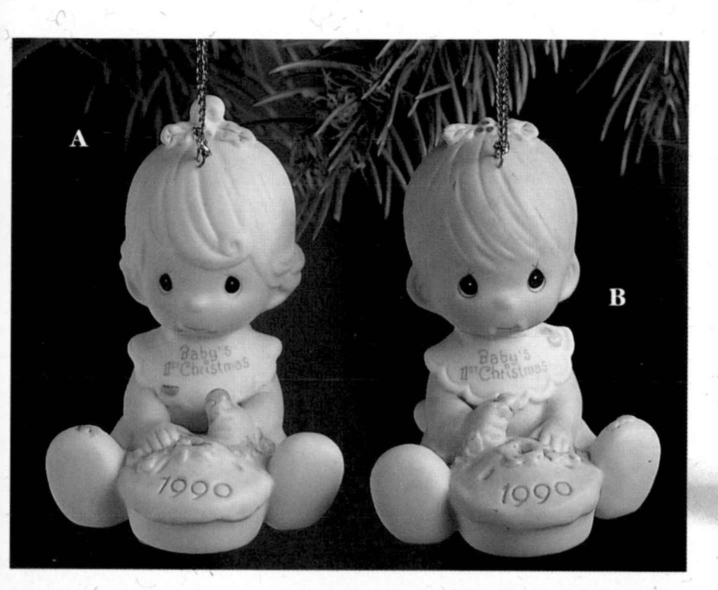

A. **Baby's First Christmas**
#523771
Dated 1990

B. **Baby's First Christmas**
#523798
Dated 1990

C. **May Your Christmas Be A Happy Home**
#523704
Dated 1990
2nd Issue In The Masterpiece Ornament Series

D. **Once Upon A Holy Night**
#523828
Dated 1990

E. **Once Upon A Holy Night**
#523852
Dated 1990

F. **Once Upon A Holy Night**
#523844
Dated 1990

G. **Once Upon A Holy Night**
#523836
Dated 1990

H. **Wishing You A Purr-fect Holiday**
#520497
Dated 1990

I. **Our First Christmas Together**
#525324
Dated 1990

A. **Oh Holy Night**
#522821
Dated 1989

B. **Oh Holy Night**
#522848
Dated 1989

C. **Oh Holy Night**
#522546
Dated 1989

D. **Oh Holy Night**
#522554
Dated 1989

E. **Christmas Is Ruff Without You**
#520462
Dated 1989

F. **Our First Christmas Together**
#521558
Dated 1989

G. **Baby's First Christmas**
#523194
Dated 1989

H. **Baby's First Christmas**
#523208
Dated 1989

I. **Peace On Earth**
#523062
Dated 1989
1st Issue In The Masterpiece Ornament Series

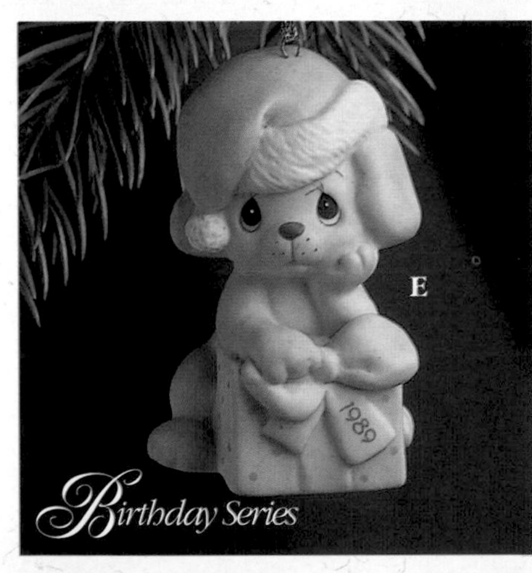

A. **Time To Wish You A Merry Christmas**
#115304
Dated 1988

B. **Time To Wish You A Merry Christmas**
#115320
Dated 1988

C. **Time To Wish You A Merry Christmas**
#115312
Dated 1988

D. **Time To Wish You A Merry Christmas**
#115339
Dated 1988

E. **Our First Christmas Together**
#520233
Dated 1988

F. **You Are My Gift Come True**
#520276
Dated 1988
1988 Limited Edition

G. **Baby's First Christmas**
#115282
Dated 1988

H. **Baby's First Christmas**
#520241
Dated 1988

I. **Hang On For The Holly Days**
#520292
Dated 1988

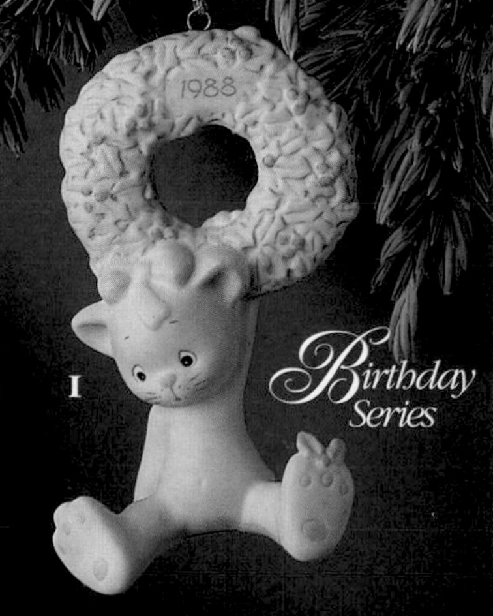

A

Birthday Series

B C D E

A. Bear The Good News Of Christmas
#104515
Dated 1987

B. Love Is The Best Gift Of All
#109835
Dated 1987

C. Love Is The Best Gift Of All
#109770
Dated 1987

D. Love Is The Best Gift Of All
#109843
Dated 1987

E. Love Is The Best Gift Of All
#110930
Dated 1987

F. Our First Christmas Together
#112399
Dated 1987

G. Baby's First Christmas
#109428
Dated 1987

H. Baby's First Christmas
#109401
Dated 1987

F G H

A. **Baby's First Christmas**
#102512
Dated 1986

B. **Baby's First Christmas**
#102504
Dated 1986

C. **Our First Christmas Together**
#102350
Dated 1986

D. **Wishing You A Cozy Christmas**
#102342
Dated 1986

E. **Wishing You A Cozy Christmas**
#102326
Dated 1986

F. **Wishing You A Cozy Christmas**
#102334
Dated 1986

G. **Wishing You A Cozy Christmas**
#102318
Dated 1986

H. **Bear On Reindeer**
#102466
Dated 1986

A
B
C
D
G
H
K
L
M

Retired Collectibles

There comes a time when certain beloved Precious Moments figurines earn a place on the honor roll of retirements. Collectors fortunate enough to have these pieces, which will never be made again, treasure them; those who don't keep searching for a favorite.

A. **To Thee With Love**
#E0534 Retired 1989

B. **To Be With You Is Uplifting**
#522260 Retired 1994

C. **Thee I Love**
#E3116 Retired 1994

D. **Someday My Love**
#520799 Retired 1992

E. **I'm So Glad You Fluttered Into My Life**
#520640 Retired 1991

F. **Our First Christmas Together**
#101702 Retired 1992
Tune: "We Wish You A Merry Christmas"

G. **Dropping Over For Christmas**
#E2375 Retired 1991

H. **Many Moons In Same Canoe, Blessum You**
#520772 Retired 1990

I. **Wishing You A Season Filled With Joy**
#E2805 Retired 1985

J. **Blessing From Above**
#523747 Retired 1994

K. **I'm Sending You A White Christmas**
#112402 Retired 1993
Tune: "White Christmas"

L. **Friendship Grows When You Plant A Seed**
#524271 Retired 1994

M. **Love Lifted Me**
#E1375A Retired 1993

N. **Christmastime Is For Sharing**
#E0504 Retired 1990

E

F

I

J

N

A. **Sharing Our Season Together**
#E0519 Retired 1986
Tune: "Winter Wonderland"

B. **Lord, Help Us Keep Our Act Together**
#101850 Retired 1992

C. **Love Is Kind**
#E5377 Retired 1987

D. **Let Love Reign**
#E9273 Retired 1987

E. **Baby's First Picture**
#E2841 Retired 1986
2nd Issue In The Baby's First Series

F. **Mother Sew Dear**
#E2850 Retired 1985

G. **Love Is Sharing**
#E7185 Retired 1985
Tune: "School Days"

H. **Loving Is Sharing**
#E3110B Retired 1993

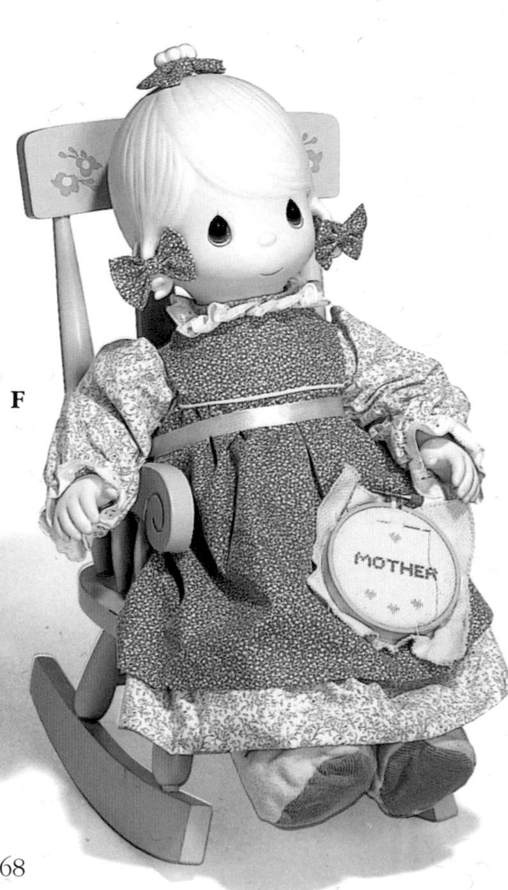

A. Bundles Of Joy
#E2374 Retired 1993

B. Surrounded With Joy
#E0506 Retired 1989

C. Glide Through The Holidays
#521566 Retired 1992

D. Dropping In For Christmas
#E2369 Retired 1986

E. Dropping Over For Christmas
#E2376 Retired 1985

F. Unicorn Hanging Ornament
#E2371 Retired 1988

G. Sending You Showers Of Blessings
#520683 Retired 1992

H. Smile Along The Way
#101842 Retired 1991

I. Showers Of Blessings
#105945 Retired 1993

J. Happiness Divine
#109584 Retired 1992

A. **O, How I Love Jesus**
#E1380B Retired 1984

B. **God Understands**
#E5211 Retired 1984

C. **I Believe In Miracles**
#E7156R Retired 1992
(Formerly E7156 Suspended)

D. **Smile, God Loves You**
#E1373B Retired 1984

E. **There Is Joy In Serving Jesus**
#E7157 Retired 1986

F. **His Eye Is On The Sparrow**
#E0530 Retired 1987

G. **God Loveth A Cheerful Giver**
#E1378 Retired 1981

H. **Praise The Lord Anyhow**
#E1374B Retired 1982

I. **I'm A Possibility**
#100188 Retired 1993

J. **Faith Is A Victory**
#521396 Retired 1993

K. **Scent From Above**
#100528 Retired 1991

L. **Blessed Are The Peacemakers**
#E3107 Retired 1985

A. **Let Heaven And Nature Sing**
#E0532 Retired 1986

B. **Joy To The World**
#E5388 Retired 1987

C. **We Have Seen His Star**
#E6120 Retired 1984

D. **The First Noël**
#E2368 Retired 1984

E. **Rejoice O Earth**
#617334 Retired 1991
Tune: "Hark, The Herald Angels Sing"

F. **Rejoice O Earth**
#113980 Retired 1991

G. **Rejoice O Earth**
#E5645 Retired 1988
Tune: "Joy To The World"

H. **O Come All Ye Faithful**
#E2353 Retired 1986

I. **Come Let Us Adore Him**
#E2011 Retired 1981

J. **Jesus Is The Light**
#E1373G Retired 1988

K. **Christmas Is A Time To Share**
#E2806 Retired 1984
Tune: "Away In A Manger"

A. Lord, Keep Me On My Toes
#100129 Retired 1988

B. Lord, Keep Me On My Toes
#102423 Retired 1990

C. Nobody's Perfect
#E9268 Retired 1990

D. Help, Lord, I'm In A Spot
#100269 Retired 1989

E. The Lord Will Carry You Through
#12467 Retired 1988
3rd Issue In The Clown Series

F. God's Speed
#E3112 Retired 1983

G. You Can't Run Away From God
#E0525 Retired 1989

H. Praise The Lord Anyhow
#E9254 Retired 1994

I. Be Not Weary In Well Doing
#E3111 Retired 1985

J. Waddle I Do Without You
#12459 Retired 1989
2nd Issue In The Clown Series

H

FRIDAY
10
Dear Sir
Bills
total

A. **Make Me A Blessing**
#100102 Retired 1990

B. **The Spirit Is Willing, But The Flesh Is Weak**
#100196 Retired 1991

C. **Eggs Over Easy**
#E3118 Retired 1983

D. **This Is Your Day To Shine**
#E2822 Retired 1988

E. **Don't Let The Holidays Get You Down**
#522112 Retired 1993

F. **Don't Let The Holidays Get You Down**
#521590 Retired 1994

G. **His Burden Is Light**
#E1380G Retired 1984

H. **God Sent You Just In Time**
#15504 Retired 1989
Tune: "We Wish You A Merry Christmas"

I. **Taste And See That The Lord Is Good**
#E9274 Retired 1986

Gene Freedman says Club members are "the most wonderful people in the world!"

A

Share the fun, join the Club

When you join the Enesco Precious Moments Collectors' Club, you receive a special Limited Edition figurine, plus

- *A twelve-month subscription to the quarterly Club magazine, The* Goodnewsletter
- *The official Gift Registry illustrated guide to the complete collection*
- *A Club binder and window decal*
- *A personal membership card*
- *The opportunity to acquire exclusive Members Only figurines*
- *All included in your $26 annual dues*

Many couples enjoy collecting and attending Club events together.

Precious Moments Collectors' Club

Sharing the joy of collecting with others is one of the benefits of membership in the Enesco Precious Moments Collectors' Club. Sharing the fulfillment of helping others is another benefit of membership. Most of all, being a Club member means coming together to share life's experiences with old friends, and making new ones. It's a club built on friendships, not memberships. Belonging creates memories that will last forever.

A. **You Are The End Of My Rainbow**
#PM041
1994 Members Only Ornament

B. **You Are The End Of My Rainbow**
#C0014
1994 Symbol of Membership Figurine
#C0114
1994 Charter Symbol Of Membership Figurine

B

A. **Loving**
#PM932
1993 Members Only Figurine

B. **Caring**
#PM941
1994 Members Only Figurine

C. **Sharing**
#PM942
1994 Members Only Figurine

D. **Members Only Medallions**
"Loving"; "Caring"; "Sharing"
#PCC112

A. **Loving, Caring, And Sharing Along The Way**
#C0013
1993 Symbol Of Membership Figurine
#C0113
1993 Charter Symbol of Membership Figurine

B. **Loving, Caring, And Sharing Along The Way**
#PM040
1993 Members Only Limited Edition Hanging Ornament

C. **His Little Treasure**
#PM931
1993 Members Only Figurine

D. **Only Love Can Make A Home**
#PM921
1992 Members Only Figurine

E. **Sowing The Seeds Of Love**
#PM922
1992 Members Only Figurine

F. **The Club That's Out Of This World**
#C0012
1992 Symbol Of Membership Figurine
#C0112
1992 Charter Symbol of Membership Figurine

G. **This Land Is Our Land**
#527386
1992 Members Only Limited Edition Figurine

A. **One Step At A Time**
#PM911
1991 Members Only Figurine

B. **Lord Keep Me In Teepee Top Shape**
#PM912
1991 Members Only Figurine

C. **Sharing The Good News Together**
#C0011
1991 Symbol Of Membership Figurine
#C0111
1991 Charter Symbol Of Membership Figurine

D. **Ten Years And Still Going Strong**
#PM901
1990 Members Only Figurine

E. **You Are A Blessing To Me**
#PM902
1990 Members Only Figurine

F. **My Happiness**
#C0010
1990 Symbol Of Membership Figurine
#C0110
1990 Charter Symbol Of Membership Figurine

A. #PM903
1990 Members Only Needlepoint Pillow

B. **Celebrating A Decade Of Loving, Caring, And Sharing**
#227986
1990 Members Only Ornament

C. #PM032
1990 Members Only Mug

D. #PM034
1990 Members Only Desk Flag

E. **Blessed Are The Poor In Spirit, For Theirs Is The Kingdom Of Heaven**
#PM190
1990 Members Only Ornament

F. **Blessed Are They That Mourn, For They Shall Be Comforted**
#PM290
1990 Members Only Ornament

G. **Blessed Are The Meek, For They Shall Inherit The Earth**
#PM390
1990 Members Only Ornament

H. **Blessed Are The Pure In Heart, For They Shall See God**
#PM690
1990 Members Only Ornament

I. **Blessed Are The Merciful, For They Shall Obtain Mercy**
#PM590
1990 Members Only Ornament

J. **Blessed Are They That Hunger And Thirst, For They Shall Be Filled**
#PM490
1990 Members Only Ornament

K. **Blessed Are The Peacemakers, For They Shall Be Called Sons Of God**
#PM790
1990 Members Only Ornament

Chapel Window Ornaments
#PM890
1990 Members Only 7 PC Assortment

A. **Mow Power To Ya**
#PM892
1989 Members Only Figurine

B. **Always Room For One More**
#C0009
1989 Symbol Of Membership Figurine
#C0109
1989 Charter Symbol Of Membership Figurine

C. **You Will Always Be My Choice**
#PM891
1989 Members Only Figurine

D. **A Growing Love**
#E0008
1988 Symbol Of Membership Figurine
#E0108
1988 Charter Symbol Of Membership Figurine

E. **God Bless You For Touching My Life**
#PM881
1988 Members Only Figurine

F. **You Just Cannot Chuck A Good Friendship**
#PM882
1988 Members Only Figurine

A. **Loving You Dear Valentine**
#PM874
1987 Members Only Figurine

B. **Feed My Sheep**
#PM871
1987 Members Only Figurine

C. **Sharing Is Universal**
#E0007
1987 Symbol Of Membership Figurine
#E0107
1987 Charter Symbol Of Membership Figurine

D. **In His Time**
#PM872
1987 Members Only Figurine

E. **Loving You Dear Valentine**
#PM873
1987 Members Only Figurine

F. **Birds Of A Feather Collect Together**
#E0006
1986 Symbol Of Membership Figurine
#E0106
1986 Charter Symbol Of Membership Figurine

G. **I'm Following Jesus**
#PM863
1986 Members Only Mug

H. **I'm Following Jesus**
#PM862
1986 Members Only Figurine

I. **Grandma's Prayer**
#PM861
1986 Members Only Figurine

This adorable figurine is yours to enjoy when you join the Enesco Precious Moments Birthday Club. You would expect to pay more than $25 for this charming porcelain bisque figurine. However, when you join the Enesco Precious Moments Birthday Club it is included, at no additional charge, in the one-year Birthday Club membership dues of only $19.

Birthday Club benefits include:

- A twelve-month subscription to *Good News Parade,* the fun-to-read Birthday Club publication
- A special "Happy Birthday" card in celebration of your special day
- The opportunity to acquire exclusive Birthday Club figurines
- A certificate of membership

Kids love meeting the Precious Moments costumed characters.

Special childrens' activities like coloring contests are always a hit at special events.

Precious Moments Birthday Club

For Kids Of All Ages

For young collectors and their families, there is the Enesco Precious Moments Birthday Club, a fun-filled club especially for children. Discovering the joys of collecting and sharing their growing years with others, young Birthday Club members learn about their world and about all God's creatures in their very own newsletter. Sharing and caring makes Birthday Club membership a loving gift for kids—from newborns to ninety-year-olds. You're never too old to enjoy a precious moment of fun!

A

B

A. **Can't Get Enough Of Our Club**
#B0009 New Introduction
1994 Symbol Of Membership Figurine
#B0109 New Introduction
1994 Charter Symbol Of Membership Figurine

B. **God Bless Our Home**
#BC941 New Introduction
1994 Members Only Figurine

A

A. **Happiness Is Belonging**
#B0008
1993 Symbol of Membership Figurine
#B0108
1993 Charter Symbol of Membership Figurine

B. **Put A Little Punch In Your Birthday**
#BC931
1993 Members Only Figurine

C. **Owl Always Be Your Friend**
#BC932
1993 Members Only Figurine

A. **I Got You Under My Skin**
#BC922
1992 Members Only Figurine

B. **Every Man's House Is His Castle**
#BC921
1992 Members Only Figurine

C. **All Aboard For Birthday Club Fun**
#B0007
1992 Symbol Of Membership Figurine
#B0107
1992 Charter Symbol Of Membership Figurine

D. **Love Pacifies**
#BC911
1991 Members Only Figurine

E. **True Blue Friends**
#BC912
1991 Members Only Figurine

F. **Jest To Let You Know You're Tops**
#B0006
1991 Symbol Of Membership Figurine
#B0106
1991 Charter Symbol Of Membership Figurine

A. **Our Club Is A Tough Act To Follow**
#B0005
1990 Symbol Of Membership Figurine
#B0105
1990 Charter Symbol Of Membership Figurine

B. **Collecting Makes Good Scents**
#BC901
1990 Members Only Figurine

C. **I'm Nuts Over My Collection**
#BC902
1990 Members Only Figurine

D. **Have A Beary Special Birthday**
#B0004
1989 Symbol Of Membership Figurine
#B0104
1989 Charter Symbol Of Membership Figurine

E. **Can't Bee Hive Myself Without You**
#BC891
1989 Members Only Figurine

A. **Somebunny Carcs**
#BC881
1988 Members Only Figurine

B. **The Sweetest Club Around**
#B0003
1988 Symbol Of Membership Figurine
#B0103
1988 Charter Symbol Of Membership Figurine

C. **A Smile's The Cymbal Of Joy**
#B0002
1987 Symbol Of Membership Figurine
#B0102
1987 Charter Symbol Of Membership Figurine

D. **Hi Sugar**
#BC871
1987 Members Only Figurine

E. **Fishing For Friends**
#BC861
1986 Members Only Figurine

F. **Our Club Can't Be Beat**
#B0001
1986 Charter Symbol Of Membership Figurine

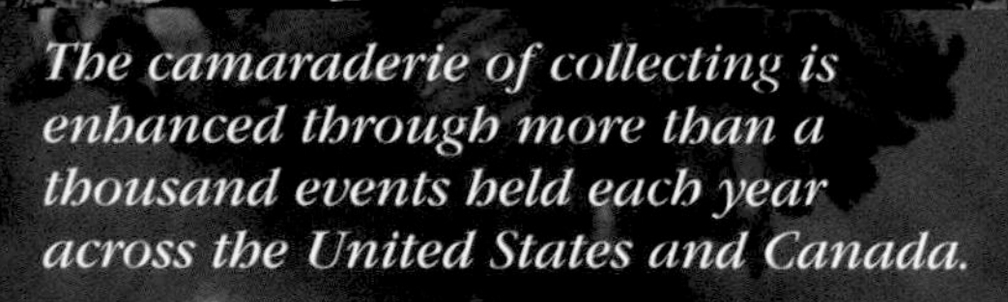

The camaraderie of collecting is enhanced through more than a thousand events held each year across the United States and Canada.

National and local events bring collectors together to enjoy seminars, entertainment, and wholesome fellowship. Each year a Limited Edition Special Event figurine is created to commemorate these happy times.

A. **Sharing Begins In The Heart**
#520861
1989 Limited Edition

B. **I'm A Precious Moments Fan**
#523526
1990 Limited Edition

C. **You Can Always Bring A Friend**
#527122
1991 Limited Edition

D. **You Are My Main Event**
#115231
1988 Limited Edition

E. **Memories Are Made Of This**
#529982
1994 Limited Edition

F. **The Magic Starts With You**
#529648
1992 Limited Edition

G. **An Event For All Seasons**
#529974
1993 Limited Edition

H. **Take A Bow Cuz You're My Christmas Star**
#520470
1994 Limited Edition

I. **Bundles Of Joy**
#525057
1990 Limited Edition

J. **An Event Worth Wading For**
#527319
1992 Limited Edition

K. **An Event For All Seasons**
#530158
1993 Limited Edition

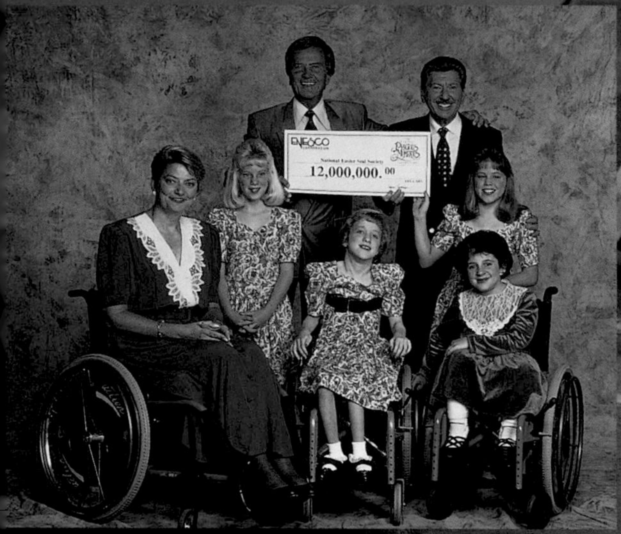

National spokesman and telethon co-host Pat Boone, with Eugene Freedman, President of Enesco, 1994 National Easter Seal adult representative Elizabeth Worstell, National Easter Seal child representatives Brandy, Amanda, and Cristy Jones, and National Easter Seal youth representative Colleen Flanagan.

A

E

F

G

Easter Seals®

Easter Seal Society

Each year artist Sam Butcher designs two Limited Edition Precious Moments figurines that play an important role in generating Easter Seal contributions. We invite you to be part of this program to support Easter Seals . . . because wonderful things happen when you "**Give Ability A Chance**."

A. **You're My Number One Friend**
#530026
1993 Commemorative Easter Seal Figurine

B. **Sharing A Gift Of Love**
#527114
1991 Commemorative Easter Seal Figurine

C. **Take Time To Smell The Flowers**
#524387 New Introduction
1995 Commemorative Easter Seal Figurine

D. **A Universal Love**
#527173
1992 Commemorative Easter Seal Figurine

E. **He Walks With Me**
#107999
1987 Commemorative Easter Seal Figurine

F. **Always In His Care**
#524522
1990 Commemorative Easter Seal Figurine

G. **His Love Will Shine On You**
#522376
1989 Commemorative Easter Seal Figurine

H. **Blessed Are They That Overcome**
#115479
1988 Commemorative Easter Seal Figurine

I. **It Is No Secret What God Can Do**
#531111
1994 Commemorative Easter Seal Figurine

9" Limited Edition Figurines

A. **You Have Touched So Many Hearts**
#523283
1990 Limited Edition of 2,000

B. **We Are God's Workmanship**
#523879
1991 Limited Edition of 2,000

C. **Make A Joyful Noise**
#520322
1989 Limited Edition of 1,500

D. **He's Got The Whole World In His Hands**
#526886
1995 Limited Edition of 2,000

D

1993 Easter Seal Child representative Palani Thies visiting one of the many Easter Seal camps for children.

Local Club Chapters give generously of their time to work the phone banks during the annual Easter Seal Telethon.

A. **Gather Your Dreams**
#529680
1993 Limited Edition of 2,000

B. **You Are The Rose Of His Creation**
#531243 New Introduction
1994 Limited Edition of 2,000

C. **Jesus Loves Me**
#104531
1988 Limited Edition of 1,000

D. **You Are Such A Purr-fect Friend**
#526010
1992 Limited Edition of 2,000

Page numbers in *italics* refer to illustrations.

Catalog Index

Title	Description	Item #	SRP	Page
Dropping Over For Christmas	Figurine	E2375	45.00	266
Dropping Over For Christmas	Ornament	E2376	10.00	269
Dusty	Figurine	529176	22.50	179
Dusty	Figurine	529435	17.00	220
Easter's On Its Way	Figurine	521892	65.00	200
Eggs Over Easy	Figurine	E3118	15.00	273
Eggspecially For You	Figurine	520667	50.00	200
Elephants	Figurine	530131	18.00	203
Especially For Ewe	Figurine	E9282C	13.50	177
Every Man's House Is His Castle	Figurine	BC921	16.50	287
Faith Is A Victory	Figurine	521396	27.50	270
Faith Takes The Plunge	Figurine	111155	35.00	194
February	Figurine	109991	35.00	208
Feed My Sheep	Figurine	PM871	25.00	281
15 Happy Years Together What A Tweet	Figurine	530786	100.00	130
15 Years Tweet Music Together	Ornament	530840	15.00	130
Fishing For Friends	Figurine	BC861	10.00	289
Flower Girl	Figurine	E2835	17.00	147
For God So Loved The World	Figurine	E5382	70.00	243
Forever Friends	Box	E9283	17.00	176
Forgiving Is Forgetting	Figurine	E9252	47.50	143
Four Seasons	Thimble	100641	20.00	211
Free Christmas Puppies	Figurine	528064	12.50	219
Friends Never Drift Apart	Figurine	100250	55.00	137
Friends Never Drift Apart	Ornament	522937	17.50	248
Friends To The End	Figurine	104418	18.50	172
Friends To The Very End	Figurine	526150	40.00	133
Friendship Grows When You Plant A Seed	Figurine	524271	40.00	267
Friendship Hits The Spot	Figurine	520748	65.00	134
Gather Your Dreams	Figurine	529680		295
Get Into The Habit Of Prayer	Figurine	12203	19.00	190
Giraffes	Figurine	530115	16.00	203
Glide Through The Holidays	Ornament	521566	13.50	269
Goat	Figurine	E2364	15.00	238
God Bless America	Figurine	102938	30.00	206
God Bless Our Family	Figurine	100498	50.00	148
God Bless Our Family	Figurine	100501	50.00	148
God Bless Our Home	Figurine	BC941	16.00	285
God Bless Our Home	Figurine	12319	60.00	164
God Bless Our Years Together	Figurine	12440	175.00	282
God Bless The Bride	Figurine	E2832	50.00	150
God Bless The Day We Found You	Figurine	100145	55.00	165
God Bless The Day We Found You	Figurine	100145R	60.00	165
God Bless The Day We Found You	Figurine	100153	55.00	165
God Bless The Day We Found You	Figurine	100153R	60.00	165
God Bless The U S A	Figurine	527564	32.50	206
God Bless You For Touching My Life	Figurine	PM881	27.50	280
God Bless You Graduate	Figurine	106194	30.00	180
God Bless You On Your Birthday	Figurine	15962	16.50	170
God Bless You With Rainbows	Nightlight	16020	57.50	184
God Blessed Our Year Together With So Much Love And Happiness	Figurine	E2854	50.00	152
God Blessed Our Years Together With So Much Love And Happiness	Figurine	E2853	50.00	152
God Blessed Our Years Together With So Much Love And Happiness	Figurine	E2855	50.00	153
God Blessed Our Years Together With So Much Love And Happiness	Figurine	E2856	50.00	153
God Blessed Our Years Together With So Much Love And Happiness	Figurine	E2857	50.00	153
God Blessed Our Years Together With So Much Love And Happiness	Figurine	E2859	50.00	153
God Blessed Our Years Together With So Much Love And Happiness	Figurine	E2860	50.00	153
God Cared Enough To Send His Best	Figurine	524476	50.00	231
God Gave His Best	Figurine	15806	19.00	229
God Is Love	Figurine	E5213	30.00	192
God Is Love Dear Valentine	Figurine	523518	30.00	145
God Is Love, Dear Valentine	Figurine	E7153	17.00	145
God Is Love, Dear Valentine	Figurine	E7154	17.00	145
God Is Love, Dear Valentine	Thimble	100625	8.00	145
God Is Watching Over You	Figurine	E7163	30.00	194
God Loveth A Cheerful Giver	Figurine	E1378	15.00	270
God Sends The Gift Of His Love	Figurine	E6613	25.00	232
God Sent His Love	Ornament	15768	10.00	262
God Sent His Love	Thimble	15865	5.50	262
God Sent His Love	Bell	15873	19.00	262
God Sent His Love	Figurine	15881	17.00	262
God Sent His Son	Figurine	E0507	37.00	240
God Sent You Just In Time	Ornament	113972	15.00	250
God Sent You Just In Time	Musical	15504	60.00	273
God Understands	Figurine	E1379B	19.00	181
God Understands	Bell	E5211	19.00	270
God's Precious Gift	Frame	12033	20.00	157
God's Precious Gift	Frame	12041	27.50	157
God's Promises Are Sure	Figurine	E9260	33.50	197
God's Ray Of Mercy	Figurine	PM841	25.00	242
God's Speed	Figurine	E3112	18.00	272
Going Home	Figurine	525979	60.00	195
Good Friends Are For Always	Figurine	524123	30.00	230
Good Friends Are For Always	Ornament	524131	16.00	248
Good Friends Are Forever	Figurine	521817	50.00	134
Good News Is So Uplifting	Figurine	523615	65.00	185
Grandfather	Figurine	529516	15.00	221
Grandma's Prayer	Figurine	PM861	25.00	281
Groom	Figurine	E2837	25.00	146
Hallelujah Country	Figurine	105821	45.00	186
Hallelujah For The Cross	Figurine	532002	35.00	197
Halo, And Merry Christmas	Figurine	12351	47.50	226
Hang On For The Holly Days	Ornament	520292	13.00	259
Happiness Divine	Figurine	109584	30.00	269
Happiness Is At Our Fingertips	Figurine	529931	35.00	132
Happiness Is Belonging	Figurine	B0008		286
Happiness Is Belonging	Figurine	B0108		286
Happiness Is The Lord	Figurine	12378	22.50	194
Happiness Is The Lord	Ornament	15830	13.50	250
Happy Birdie	Figurine	527343	16.00	173
Happy Birthday Dear Jesus	Figurine	524875	13.50	238
Happy Birthday Jesus	Figurine	530492	20.00	245
Happy Birthday Little Lamb	Figurine	15946	15.00	170
Happy Bithday Poppy	Figurine	106836	35.00	166
Happy Days Are Here Again	Figurine	104396	32.50	174
Happy Trails Is Trusting Jesus	Ornament	523224	16.00	250
Happy Trip	Figurine	521280	35.00	184
Have A Beary Merry Christmas	Figurine	522856	16.50	229
Have A Berry Special Birthday	Figurine	B0004		288
Have A Berry Special Birthday	Figurine	B0104		288
Have A Heavenly Christmas	Ornament	12416	17.50	246
Have I Got News For You	Figurine	105635	30.00	236
Have I Got News For You	Figurine	528137	16.00	244
He Careth For You	Figurine	E1377B	20.00	232
He Cleansed My Soul	Figurine	100277	37.50	194
He Cleansed My Soul	Ornament	112380	16.00	250
He Is My Song	Figurine	12394	27.50	194
He Is The Star Of The Morning	Figurine	522252	60.00	243
He Leadeth Me	Figurine	E1377A	20.00	232
He Loves Me	Figurine	524263	35.00	198
He Upholdeth Those Who Fall	Figurine	E0526	35.00	197
He Walks With Me	Figurine	107999	25.00	292
He Watches Over Us All	Figurine	E3105	17.00	292
He's Got The Whole World In His Hands	Figurine	526886		294
He's The Healer Of Broken Hearts	Figurine	100080	50.00	143
Heaven Bless You	Musical	100285	60.00	155
Heaven Bless You	Figurine	520934	35.00	155
Heaven Bless Your Special Day	Figurine	15954	16.50	170
Heaven Bless Your Togetherness	Figurine	106755	90.00	151
Hello World	Figurine	521175	16.00	172
Hello, Lord, It's Me Again	Figurine	PM811	25.00	283
Help, Lord, I'm In A Spot	Figurine	100269	25.00	272
Hi Sugar	Figurine	BC871	11.00	289
High Hopes	Figurine	521957	30.00	187
His Burden Is Light	Figurine	E1380G	19.00	273
His Eye Is On The Sparrow	Figurine	E0530	32.50	270
His Little Treasure	Figurine	PM931	30.00	277
His Love Will Shine On You	Figurine	522376	30.00	292
His Name Is Jesus	Figurine	E5381	50.00	242
His Sheep Am I	Figurine	E7161	27.50	240
Holy Smokes	Figurine	E2351	33.50	227
Honk If You Love Jesus	Figurine	15490	20.00	239
Honk If You Love Jesus	Ornament	15857	15.00	250
Hope You're Over The Hump	Figurine	521671	17.50	172
Hope You're Up And On The Trail Again	Figurine	521205	35.00	188
Hoppy Easter, Friend	Figurine	521906	40.00	200
How Can I Ever Forget You	Figurine	526924	16.00	172
How Can Two Walk Together Except They Agree	Figurine	E9263	35.00	142
Hug One Another	Figurine	521299	50.00	138
I Believe In Miracles	Figurine	E7156	19.00	270
I Believe In Miracles	Figurine	E7156R	27.50	270
I Believe In Miracles	Plate	E9257	40.00	193
I Believe In The Old Rugged Cross	Figurine	103632	35.00	192
I Believe In The Old Rugged Cross	Ornament	522953	16.00	250
I Belong To The Lord	Figurine	520853	27.50	196
I Can't Spell Success Without You	Figurine	523763	45.00	187
I Can't Bear To Let You Go	Figurine	532037	50.00	141
I Get A Bang Out Of You	Figurine	12262	45.00	176
I Get A Kick Out Of You	Figurine	E2827	50.00	136
I Got You Under My Skin	Figurine	BC922	16.00	287
I Love To Tell The Story	Figurine	PM852	27.50	282
I Only Have Arms For You	Figurine	527769	16.00	173
I Picked A Very Special Mom	Figurine	100536	40.00	167
I Still Do	Figurine	530999	30.00	152
I Still Do	Figurine	531006	30.00	152
I Will Always Be Thinking Of You	Figurine	523631	45.00	136
I Will Cherish The Old Rugged Cross	Egg	523534	27.50	201
I Would Be Lost Without You	Figurine	526142	30.00	187
I Would Be Sunk Without You	Figurine	102970	19.00	160
I'll Never Stop Loving You	Figurine	521418	37.50	139
I'll Play My Drum For Him	Musical	E2355	50.00	240
I'll Play My Drum For Him	Figurine	E2356	33.00	240
I'll Play My Drum For Him	Plate	E2357	40.00	265
I'll Play My Drum For Him	Bell	E2358	17.00	264
I'll Play My Drum For Him	Ornament	E2359	9.00	251
I'll Play My Drum For Him	Figurine	E2360	25.00	236
I'll Play My Drum For Him	Figurine	E5384	16.00	245
I'm A Possibility	Figurine	100188	35.00	270
I'm A Possibility	Ornament	111120	15.00	250
I'm A Precious Moments Fan	Figurine	523526	25.00	290
I'm Falling For Some Bunny And It Happens To Be You	Box	E9266	18.50	176
I'm Following Jesus	Figurine	PM862	25.00	281
I'm Following Jesus	Mug	PM863	17.50	281
I'm Nuts About You	Ornament	520411	16.00	255
I'm Nuts Over My Collection	Figurine	BC902	15.00	288
I'm Sending You A White Christmas	Figurine	E2829	50.00	226
I'm Sending You A White Christmas	Plate	101834	45.00	265
I'm Sending You A White Christmas	Ornament	112372	15.00	247
I'm Sending You A White Christmas	Musical	112402	75.00	266
I'm So Glad That God Has Blessed Me With A Friend Like You	Figurine	523623	50.00	132
I'm So Glad You Fluttered Into My Life	Figurine	520640	45.00	266
If God Be For Us, Who Can Be Against Us?	Figurine	E9285	27.50	198
In His Time	Figurine	PM872	25.00	281
In The Spotlight Of His Grace	Figurine	520543	35.00	193
Isn't Eight Just Great	Figurine	109460	22.50	171
Isn't He Precious	Figurine	E5379	30.00	239
Isn't He Precious	Figurine	522988	16.50	245
Isn't He Wonderful	Figurine	E5639	17.00	238
Isn't He Wonderful	Figurine	E5640	17.00	238
It Is Better To Give Than To Receive	Figurine	12297	21.00	187
It Is No Secret What God Can Do	Figurine	531111	30.00	293
It's A Perfect Boy	Figurine	E0512	27.50	239
It's A Perfect Boy	Ornament	102415	13.50	249

Title	Description	Item #	SRP	Page
Nativity Buildings & Tree	Figurine	E2387	75.00	244
Nativity Cart	Figurine	528072	18.50	237
Nativity Wall	Figurine	E5644	120.00	236
No Tears Past The Gate	Figurine	101826	65.00	195
Noah's Ark	Figurine	530042	125.00	202
Nobody's Perfect	Figurine	E9268	30.00	272
Not A Creature Was Stirring	Figurine	524484	17.00	172
Nothing Can Dampen The Spirit Of Caring	Figurine	603864	35.00	204
November	Figurine	110108	37.50	209
Now I Lay Me Down To Sleep	Figurine	522058	30.00	226
O Come All Ye Faithful	Ornament	E0531	10.00	251
O Come All Ye Faithful	Musical	E2352	50.00	231
O Come All Ye Faithful	Figurine	E2353	30.00	271
O Come, Let Us Adore Him	Figurine	111333	220.00	241
O Worship The Lord	Figurine	100064	35.00	199
O Worship The Lord	Figurine	102229	35.00	199
O, How I Love Jesus	Figurine	E1380B	19.00	270
October	Figurine	110094	45.00	208
Oh Holy Night	Figurine	522546	25.00	258
Oh Holy Night	Thimble	522554	7.50	258
Oh Holy Night	Bell	522821	25.00	258
Oh Holy Night	Ornament	522848	13.50	258
Oh What Fun It Is To Ride	Figurine	109819	110.00	224
Oh Worship The Lord	Figurine	E5385	10.00	232
Oh Worship The Lord	Figurine	E5386	10.00	232
Oinky Birthday	Figurine	524506	13.50	173
Once Upon A Holy Night	Bell	523828	25.00	257
Once Upon A Holy Night	Figurine	523836	25.00	257
Once Upon A Holy Night	Thimble	523844	8.00	257
Once Upon A Holy Night	Ornament	523852	15.00	257
One Step At A Time	Figurine	PM911	33.00	278
Only Love Can Make A Home	Figurine	PM921	30.00	277
Onward Christian Soldiers	Figurine	E0523	35.00	192
Onward Christmas Soldiers	Ornament	527327	16.00	251
Our Club Can't Be Beat	Figurine	B0001		289
Our Club Is A Tough Act To Follow	Figurine	B0005		288
Our Club Is A Tough Act To Follow	Figurine	B0105		288
Our First Christmas Together	Figurine	E2377	37.50	228
Our First Christmas Together	Plate	E2378	30.00	228
Our First Christmas Together	Ornament	E2385	15.00	248
Our First Christmas Together	Musical	101702	70.00	266
Our First Christmas Together	Ornament	102350	10.00	261
Our First Christmas Together	Ornament	112399	11.00	260
Our First Christmas Together	Figurine	115290	60.00	228
Our First Christmas Together	Ornament	520233	13.00	259
Our First Christmas Together	Ornament	521558	17.50	258
Our First Christmas Together	Ornament	522945	17.50	256
Our First Christmas Together	Ornament	525324	17.50	257
Our First Christmas Together	Ornament	528870	17.50	255
Our First Christmas Together	Ornament	529206	18.50	252
Our First Christmas Together	Ornament	530506	17.50	254
Our Friendship Is Soda-licious	Figurine	524336	65.00	134
Our Love Is Heaven Scent	Box	E9266	18.50	176
Owl Always Be Your Friend	Figurine	BC932	16.00	286
P.D.	Doll	12475	50.00	214
Part Of Me Wants To Be Good	Figurine	12149	25.00	166
Peace Amid The Storm	Figurine	E4723	27.50	205
Peace On Earth	Figurine	E2804	27.50	234
Peace On Earth	Figurine	E4725	30.00	235
Peace On Earth	Musical	E4726	50.00	235
Peace On Earth	Ornament	E5389	10.00	251
Peace On Earth	Figurine	E9287	37.50	235
Peace On Earth	Musical	109746	130.00	235
Peace On Earth	Ornament	523062	25.00	258
Perfect Harmony	Figurine	521914	55.00	234
Philip	Figurine	529494	17.00	221
Pigs	Figurine	530085	12.00	202
Praise The Lord Anyhow	Figurine	E1374B	17.00	270
Praise The Lord Anyhow	Figurine	E9254	55.00	272
Prayer Changes Things	Figurine	E1375B	22.50	190
Prayer Changes Things	Bell	E5210	19.00	190
Prayer Changes Things	Figurine	E5214	37.50	191
Precious Memories	Figurine	E2828	65.00	151
Precious Memories	Figurine	106763	50.00	152
Prepare Ye The Way Of The Lord	Figurine	E0508	75.00	242
Press On	Figurine	E9265	60.00	188
Puppy Love	Figurine	520764	16.00	144
Puppy Love Is From Above	Figurine	106798	55.00	152
Put A Little Punch In Your Birthday	Figurine	BC931	15.00	286
Put On A Happy Face	Figurine	PM822	25.00	283
Reindeer	Ornament	102466	11.00	261
Rejoice O Earth	Figurine	E5636	30.00	237
Rejoice O Earth	Musical	E5645	55.00	271
Rejoice O Earth	Ornament	113980	15.00	271
Rejoice O Earth	Figurine	520268	16.00	244
Rejoice O Earth	Tree Topper	617334	125.00	271
Rejoicing With You	Figurine	E4724	50.00	155
Rejoicing With You	Plate	E7172	30.00	154
Ring Bearer	Figurine	E2833	17.00	147
Ring Out The Good News	Figurine	529966	27.50	233
Ring Those Christmas Bells	Figurine	525898	95.00	225
Rocking Horse	Ornament	102474	15.00	249
Safe In The Arms Of Jesus	Figurine	521922	30.00	157
Sam Butcher	Figurine	529567	22.50	221
Sam Butcher	Figurine	529842	22.50	220
Sam's Car	Figurine	529443	22.50	220
Sam's House	Nightlight	529605	80.00	220
Sam's House	Ornament	530468	17.50	218
Sam's House Collector's Set	Figurine	531774	189.00	220
Sammy	Figurine	528668	17.00	220
Sammy	Figurine	529222	20.00	178
Sammy's Circus Collector's Set	Figurine	604070	200.00	178
Scent From Above	Figurine	100528	27.50	270
Sealed With A Kiss	Figurine	524441	50.00	150
Seek And Ye Shall Find	Figurine	E0005		282
Seek And Ye Shall Find	Figurine	E0105		282
Seek Ye The Lord	Figurine	E9261	21.00	183
Seek Ye The Lord	Figurine	E9262	21.00	183
Sending My Love	Figurine	100056	32.50	144
Sending My Love Your Way	Figurine	528609	40.00	139
Sending You A Rainbow	Figurine	E9288	22.50	184
Sending You A White Christmas	Ornament	528218	16.00	246
Sending You My Love	Figurine	109967	45.00	144
Sending You Oceans Of Love	Figurine	532010	35.00	138
Sending You Showers Of Blessings	Figurine	520683	35.00	269
September	Figurine	110086	35.00	208
Serenity Prayer Boy	Figurine	530700	35.00	190
Serenity Prayer Girl	Figurine	530697	35.00	190
Serve With A Smile	Ornament	102431	12.50	250
Serve With A Smile	Ornament	102458	12.50	250
Serving The Lord	Figurine	100161	27.50	198
Serving The Lord	Figurine	100293	27.50	198
Sew In Love	Figurine	106844	55.00	139
Share In The Warmth Of Christmas	Ornament	527211	16.00	246
Sharing	Figurine	PM942	35.00	276
Sharing A Gift Of Love	Figurine	527114	30.00	293
Sharing Begins In The Heart	Figurine	520861	25.00	290
Sharing Is Universal	Figurine	E0007		281
Sharing Is Universal	Figurine	E0107		281
Sharing Our Christmas Together	Figurine	102490	45.00	228
Sharing Our Joy Together	Figurine	E2834	40.00	150
Sharing Our Season Together	Figurine	E0501	50.00	228
Sharing Our Season Together	Musical	E0519	70.00	268
Sharing Sweet Moments Together	Figurine	526487	45.00	144
Sharing The Good News Together	Figurine	C0011		278
Sharing The Good News Together	Figurine	C0111		278
Sheep	Figurine	530077	10.00	202
Shepherd Of Love	Figurine	102261	16.00	245
Shepherd Of Love	Ornament	102288	15.00	251
Showers Of Blessings	Figurine	105945	20.00	269
Silent Knight	Musical	E5642	60.00	231
Silent Night	Musical	15814	55.00	229
Sitting Pretty	Figurine	104825	30.00	161
Slow Down And Enjoy The Holidays	Ornament	520489	16.00	254
Smile Along The Way	Figurine	101842	45.00	269
Smile Along The Way	Ornament	113964	17.50	246
Smile, God Loves You	Figurine	E1373B	17.00	270
Smile, God Loves You	Figurine	PM821	25.00	283
Sno-bunny Falls For You Like I Do	Ornament	520438	15.00	256
So Glad I Picked You As A Friend	Figurine	524379	40.00	132
Some Bunny's Sleeping	Figurine	115274	18.50	238
Some Bunny's Sleeping	Figurine	522996	12.00	245
Somebunny Cares	Figurine	BC881	13.50	289
Someday My Love	Figurine	520799	45.00	266
Something's Missing When You're Not Around	Figurine	105643	37.50	137
Sowing The Seeds Of Love	Figurine	PM922	30.00	277
Stork With Baby Sam	Figurine	529788	22.50	218
Sugar And Her Doghouse	Figurine	533165	20.00	219
Sugar Town Chapel	Nightlight	529621	85.00	221
Sugar Town Chapel	Ornament	530484	17.50	220
Sugar Town Cobblestone Bridge	Figurine	533203	17.00	219
Sugar Town Curved Sidewalk	Figurine	533149	10.00	219
Sugar Town Doctor's Office Set	Figurine	529281	189.00	220
Sugar Town Double Tree	Figurine	533181	10.00	219
Sugar Town Evergreen Tree	Figurine	528684	15.00	221
Sugar Town Fence	Figurine	529796	10.00	220
Sugar Town Lamp Post	Figurine	529559	8.00	218
Sugar Town Mailbox	Figurine	531847	5.00	218
Sugar Town Nativity	Figurine	529508	20.00	221
Sugar Town Single Tree	Figurine	533173	10.00	219
Sugar Town Square Clock	Clock	532908	80.00	218
Sugar Town Straight Sidewalk	Figurine	533157	10.00	218
Summer's Joy	Figurine	12076	30.00	210
Summer's Joy	Plate	12114	40.00	211
Summer's Joy	Jack-in-the-box	408743	200.00	212
Summer's Joy	Doll	408794	150.00	212
Surround Us With Joy	Ornament	E0513	9.00	263
Surrounded With Joy	Figurine	E0506	27.50	269
Surrounded With Joy	Bell	E0522	18.00	263
Sweep All Your Worries Away	Figurine	521779	40.00	188
Take A Bow Cuz You're My Christmas Star	Ornament	520470	16.00	290
Take Heed When You Stand	Figurine	521272	55.00	186
Take Time To Smell The Flowers	Figurine	524387	30.00	293
Tammy	Doll	E7267G	300.00	214
Taste And See That The Lord Is Good	Figurine	E9274	22.50	273
Tell It To Jesus	Figurine	521477	37.50	190
Tell Me A Story	Figurine	15792	15.00	229
Tell Me The Story Of Jesus	Ornament	E0533	12.50	251
Tell Me The Story Of Jesus	Figurine	E2349	33.00	231
Tell Me The Story Of Jesus	Plate	15237	40.00	265
Ten Years And Still Going Strong	Figurine	PM901	30.00	278
Thank You For Coming To My Ade	Figurine	E5202	30.00	187
Thank You, Lord, For Everything	Figurine	522031	60.00	235
Thanking Him For You	Figurine	E7155	17.00	190
That's What Friends Are For	Figurine	521183	45.00	135
The Club That's Out Of This World	Figurine	C0012		277
The Club That's Out Of This World	Figurine	C0112		277
The End Is In Sight	Figurine	E9253	25.00	188
The Eyes Of The Lord Are Upon You	Musical	429570	65.00	214
The Eyes Of The Lord Are Upon You	Musical	429589	65.00	214
The First Noel	Figurine	E2365	17.00	233
The First Noel	Figurine	E2366	17.00	233
The First Noel	Ornament	E2367	10.00	251
The First Noel	Ornament	E2368	10.00	271
The Fruit Of The Spirit Is Love	Figurine	521213	30.00	228
The Good Lord Always Delivers	Figurine	523453	30.00	154
The Good Lord Always Delivers	Ornament	527165	15.00	249
The Good Lord Has Blessed Us Tenfold	Figurine	114022	90.00	164
The Greatest Gift Is A Friend	Figurine	109231	37.50	230
The Greatest Of These Is Love	Figurine	521868	30.00	192
The Hand That Rocks The Future	Figurine	E3108	19.00	156
The Hand That Rocks The Future	Musical	E5204	60.00	156

Item Number / Page Number Reference

For your convenience, the following is a list of every item number in this Precious Moments book.
Next to each item number you will find the suggested retail price, the page number on which the item is located, and year reference.

	520667	....$50.00	200	1988
	520675	....$75.00	141	1988
†	520683	....$35.00	269	1988
	520691	....$65.00	189	1990
*	520705	....$50.00	163	1988
	520721	....$75.00	136	1988
	520748	....$65.00	134	1988
	520756	....$45.00	196	1988
	520764	....$16.00	144	1988
†	520772	....$55.00	267	1988
	520780	....$75.00	151	1988
†	520799	....$45.00	266	1988
*	520802	....$70.00	136	1988
*	520810	....$37.50	135	1988
	520829	....$30.00	144	1988
	520837	....$60.00	150	1988
	520845	....$65.00	151	1988
*	520853	....$27.50	196	1988
	520861	....$25.00	290	1988
	520934	....$35.00	155	1989
	521000	....$30.00	132	1992
*	521043	....$16.00	173	1990
	521175	....$16.00	172	1988
	521183	....$45.00	135	1990
*	521205	....$35.00	188	1989
	521213	....$30.00	228	1993
*	521272	....$55.00	186	1991
*	521280	....$35.00	184	1989
	521299	....$50.00	138	1990
*	521302	....$16.00	247	1989
*	521310	....$30.00	189	1989
†	521396	....$27.50	270	1989
	521418	....$37.50	139	1989
*	521434	....$35.00	230	1991
	521450	....$35.00	188	1989
	521477	....$37.50	190	1989
	521485	....$55.00	188	1990
	521493	....$30.00	154	1991
	521507	....$70.00	233	1989
	521558	....$17.50	258	1989
†	521566	....$13.50	269	1990
*	521574	....$16.00	246	1990
†	521590	....$16.00	273	1990
	521671	....$17.50	172	1993
	521698	....$60.00	138	1990
	521779	....$40.00	188	1989
	521817	....$50.00	134	1989
	521825	....$25.00	170	1991
	521833	....$25.00	170	1991
	521841	....$45.00	141	1989
*	521868	....$30.00	192	1989
	521892	....$65.00	200	1989
	521906	....$40.00	200	1990
	521914	....$55.00	234	1994
	521922	....$30.00	157	1992
	521949	....$45.00	226	1989
*	521957	....$30.00	187	1989
	521965	....$35.00	167	1990
	522015	....$32.50	180	1993
	522023	....$50.00	189	1989
*	522031	....$60.00	235	1989
	522058	....$30.00	226	1994
	522082	....$55.00	234	1991
	522090	....$70.00	135	1989
*	522104	....$65.00	140	1991
†	522112	....$45.00	273	1989
	522120	....$70.00	227	1989
	522201	....$90.00	184	1989
*	522244	....$75.00	224	1992
*	522252	....$60.00	243	1989
†	522260	....$22.50	267	1989
	522279	....$50.00	192	1990
	522287	....$30.00	136	1989
	522317	....$60.00	224	1989
	522376	....$30.00	292	1988
	522546	....$25.00	258	1989
	522554	......$7.50	258	1989
	522821	....$25.00	258	1989
	522848	....$13.50	258	1989
*	522856	....$16.50	229	1989
	522910	....$16.00	247	1989
	522929	....$17.50	248	1989
	522937	....$17.50	248	1990
	522945	....$17.50	256	1991
*	522953	....$16.00	250	1989
*	522988	....$16.50	245	1989
*	522996	....$12.00	245	1990
	523003	....$50.00	265	1989
	523062	....$25.00	258	1989
*	523097	....$25.00	239	1989
	523178	....$50.00	154	1990
	523194	....$15.00	258	1989
	523208	....$15.00	258	1989
*	523224	....$16.00	250	1991
	523283	....	294	1989
	523453	....$30.00	154	1989
	523496	....$30.00	199	1989
	523518	....$30.00	145	1989
	523526	....$25.00	290	1990
	523534	....$27.50	201	1990
	523542	....$40.00	140	1991
	523593	....$40.00	197	1992
	523615	....$65.00	185	1991
	523623	....$50.00	132	1992
	523631	....$45.00	136	1993
	523682	....$60.00	199	1991
	523704	....$27.50	257	1990
	523739	....$37.50	188	1990
†	523747	....$50.00	266	1990
	523755	....$45.00	226	1994
*	523763	....$45.00	187	1990
	523771	....$15.00	257	1990
	523798	....$15.00	257	1990
	523801	....$50.00	264	1990
	523828	....$25.00	257	1990
	523836	....$25.00	257	1990
	523844	......$8.00	257	1990
	523852	....$15.00	257	1990
	523860	....$50.00	264	1991
	523879	....	294	1990
	524069	....$25.00	163	1992
	524077	....$37.50	162	1990
	524085	....$60.00	140	1991
	524123	....$30.00	230	1991
	524131	....$16.00	248	1992
	524158	....$35.00	204	1993
	524166	....$27.50	256	1991
	524174	....$15.00	256	1991
	524182	....$25.00	256	1991
	524190	......$8.00	256	1991
	524263	....$35.00	198	1990
†	524271	....$40.00	267	1991
	524298	....$50.00	173	1992
	524301	....$30.00	173	1990
	524336	....$65.00	134	1992
	524352	....$50.00	205	1991
	524379	....$40.00	132	1993
	524387	....$30.00	293	1994
	524395	....$35.00	132	1992
	524425	....$35.00	135	1990
	524441	....$50.00	150	1992
	524468	....$32.50	233	1993
	524476	....$50.00	231	1994
*	524484	....$17.00	172	1990
	524492	....$16.00	172	1990
	524506	....$13.50	173	1993
	524522	....$30.00	292	1989
*	524875	....$13.50	238	1990
*	524883	....$37.50	229	1990
	524905	....$40.00	230	1992
	524913	....$50.00	234	1990
	524921	....$65.00	232	1991
	525057	....$15.00	290	1989
	525278	....$10.00	245	1992
	525286	....$17.00	245	1991
	525316	....$35.00	199	1992
	525324	....$17.50	257	1990
	525332	....$16.00	250	1992
	525898	....$95.00	225	1992
	525960	....$27.50	200	1991
	525979	....$60.00	195	1991
	526010	....	295	1991
	526142	....$30.00	187	1991
	526150	....$40.00	133	1993
	526185	....$37.50	140	1991
	526193	....$35.00	140	1993
	526487	....$45.00	144	1993
*	526568	....$32.50	207	1991
*	526576	....$32.50	207	1991
*	526584	....$32.50	207	1991
	526886	....	294	1994
	526916	..$100.00	135	1992
	526924	....$16.00	172	1991
	526940	....$30.00	256	1991
*	526959	....$17.50	238	1991
	527084	....$15.00	256	1991
	527092	....$15.00	256	1991
	527114	....$30.00	293	1990
	527122	....$27.50	290	1990
*	527165	....$15.00	249	1991
	527173	....$32.50	293	1991
	527211	....$16.00	246	1993
	527238	....$25.00	163	1992
	527270	....$16.00	172	1991
*	527289	....$32.50	207	1991
*	527297	....$32.50	207	1991
	527319	....$32.50	290	1991
	527327	....$16.00	251	1994
	527335	....$35.00	195	1992
	527343	....$16.00	173	1992
	527378	....$60.00	228	1992
**	527386	..$350.00	277	1991
	527475	....$15.00	255	1992
	527483	....$15.00	255	1992
*	527521	....$32.50	206	1991
	527556	....$90.00	196	1991
	527564	....$32.50	206	1991
	527580	....$40.00	225	1993
	527599	....$45.00	224	1993
	527629	....$40.00	224	1992
	527661	....$35.00	186	1991
	527688	....$27.50	255	1992
	527696	....$15.00	255	1992
	527718	......$8.00	255	1992
	527726	....$25.00	255	1992
	527734	....$30.00	255	1992
	527742	....$50.00	264	1992
	527750	....$27.50	239	1992
	527769	....$16.00	173	1992
	527777	....$35.00	206	1991
	528064	....$12.50	219	1994
	528072	....$18.50	237	1994
	528099	....$18.50	179	1993
	528137	....$16.00	244	1994
	528196	....$90.00	178	1993
	528218	....$16.00	246	1994
	528226	....$16.00	246	1994
	528609	....$40.00	139	1994
	528617	....$27.50	201	1992
	528633	....$60.00	166	1993
	528668	....$17.00	220	1993
	528684	....$15.00	221	1992
	528846	....$16.00	248	1993
	528862	....$35.00	206	1992
	528870	....$17.50	255	1992
	529095	....$27.50	200	1993
	529176	....$22.50	179	1993
	529184	....$17.00	178	1993
	529192	....$12.00	179	1993
	529206	....$18.50	252	1994
	529214	....$20.00	178	1993
	529222	....$20.00	178	1993
	529281	..$189.00	220	1994
	529435	....$17.00	220	1992
	529443	....$22.50	220	1993
	529486	....$20.00	221	1992
	529494	....$17.00	221	1992
	529508	....$20.00	221	1992
	529516	....$15.00	221	1992
	529524	....$20.00	220	1992
	529559	......$8.00	218	1994
	529567	....$22.50	221	1992
	529605	....$80.00	220	1992
	529621	....$85.00	221	1992
	529648	....$16.00	290	1992
	529680	....	295	1992
	529788	....$22.50	218	1994
	529796	....$10.00	220	1993
	529818	....$20.00	218	1994
	529826	....$17.00	218	1994
	529842	....$22.50	220	1993
	529850	....$17.00	218	1994
	529869	....$80.00	222	1994
	529931	....$35.00	132	1992
	529966	....$27.50	233	1993
	529974	....$15.00	290	1993
	529982	....$30.00	291	1993
	530026	....$30.00	292	1992
	530042	..$125.00	202	1992
	530077	....$10.00	202	1992
	530085	....$12.00	202	1992
	530115	....$16.00	203	1992
	530123	......$9.00	202	1992
	530131	....$18.00	203	1992
	530158	....$30.00	291	1992
	530166	....$27.50	254	1993
	530174	....$25.00	254	1993
	530182	......$8.00	254	1993
	530190	....$30.00	254	1993
	530204	....$50.00	264	1993
	530212	....$15.00	254	1993
	530255	....$16.00	252	1994
	530263	....$16.00	252	1994
	530387	....$30.00	253	1994
	530395	....$16.00	252	1994
	530409	....$50.00	252	1994
	530425	....$27.50	253	1994
	530468	....$17.50	218	1994
	530484	....$17.50	220	1993
	530492	....$20.00	245	1993
	530506	....$17.50	254	1993
	530697	....$35.00	190	1993
	530700	....$35.00	190	1993
	530786	..$100.00	130	1992
	530840	....$15.00	130	1992
	530859	....$15.00	254	1993
	530867	....$15.00	254	1993
	530948	..$190.00	202	1992
	530972	....$16.00	252	1994
	530999	....$30.00	152	1993
	531006	....$30.00	152	1993
	531065	....$45.00	205	1994
	531111	....$30.00	293	1993
	531146	....$32.50	191	1994
	531243	....	295	1993
	531359	....$50.00	196	1993
	531375	....$15.00	203	1993
	531707	....$32.50	190	1993
	531766	....$50.00	167	1993
	531774	..$189.00	220	1993
	531847	......$5.00	218	1994
	531952	....$40.00	224	1994
	532002	....$35.00	197	1994
	532010	....$35.00	138	1994
	532037	....$50.00	141	1994
	532118	....$40.00	148	1993
	532126	....$30.00	180	1993
	532134	....$30.00	180	1993
	532908	....$80.00	218	1994
	532916	....$35.00	231	1994
	533149	....$10.00	219	1994
	533157	....$10.00	218	1994
	533165	....$20.00	219	1994
	533173	....$10.00	219	1994
	533181	....$10.00	219	1994
	533203	....$17.00	219	1994
	603171	....$30.00	246	1994
	603864	....$35.00	204	1993
	604070	..$200.00	178	1993
	604208	....$35.00	184	1994
	604216	....$27.50	253	1994
†	617334	..$125.00	271	1990
	770272	....$70.00	219	1994

SYMBOL KEY

- ♀ – Illuminated
- ⇄ – Action

- * Suspended
- † Retired

Collectors' Club

- ‡ Available to Charter Members
- ‡‡ Available to New Members
- ** Available to Members Only in year denoted

Birthday Club

- ★ Available to Charter Members
- ★★ Available to New Members
- ☆ Available to Members Only in year denoted